◢ *WHAT PEOPLE ARE SAYING* ABOUT KEEP THE CHANGE

Keep the Change reminds us that spiritual transformation is fundamental to our Christian faith. As we learn to rely on God's power in our lives, we experience the peace and purpose that comes from putting Him first. With wisdom from God's Word, deeply personal examples, and practical encouragement, Rob Ketterling coaches us on how to fight the good fight, finish the race, and keep the faith (2 Timothy 4:7).

Chris Hodges
Senior Pastor, Church of the Highlands
Author of *Out of the Cave* and *Pray First*

Rob's vulnerability shines through his personal stories and practical advice. Change is hard, and takes lots of effort; I'm so glad my friend Rob Ketterling wrote this book; I know it is going to help so many!

Lisa Bevere
New York Times best-selling author and minister and
Cofounder of Messenger International and MessengerX

In a culture that is always changing, this book, *Keep the Change,* will help you to understand and maintain your course. It is a must-read sequel from Rob Ketterling.

Choco De Jesús
General Treasurer, Assemblies of God
Author of *Love Them Anyway*

Many people experience change in their lives; not nearly as many 'keep the change'. Rob Ketterling's engaging book provides transforming stories and Christ-centered encouragements for finding the change you need, but especially for walking in "newness of life" through Christ every day. Buy the book and keep the change!

Robert Crosby, PhD
President/CEO Emerge Counseling Ministries
Author of *The One Jesus Loves* and *The Teaming Church*

Knowing what to change is only half the battle. Pastor Rob encourages readers to not just know what to change, but to be committed to the change. More importantly, it's not just words Rob says, but its words he lives by.

Bianca Juarez Olthoff
Pastor, podcaster, and best-selling author

Too often, people have the desire to make changes but struggle to keep their commitments. Rob's new book, *Keep the Change,* is full of powerful personal stories and packed with practical tools for sustainable life change.

Craig Groeschel
Senior Pastor of Life.Church
Author of *Lead Like It Matters*

I've had the honor of serving Pastor Rob Ketterling as his leadership and organizational consultant for many years. Almost all consults with him can be distilled to some aspect of change—personal or professional. Therefore, after years of up close interactions, I can attest that Rob Ketterling keeps the change. This book hence is authentically who Rob Ketterling is. You're not reading a book—you're journeying with the author. You too can keep the change.

Sam Chand
Leadership architect, author and consultant

KEEP THE
CHANGE

◢ **Rob Ketterling**

▰ Don't **Lose** what you've worked so hard to **Gain**

Author's note: The anecdotes throughout this book are all true, although some names have been changed to ensure anonymity for the person(s) involved.

ISBNs:
Print: 978-1-7360153-0-8
eBook: 978-0-9863320-9-8
Audio: 978-1-7360153-1-5

Cover design by Annie Judd
Interior formatting by Anne McLaughlin, Blue Lake Design
Published by River Valley Resources

Printed in the United States

◢ CONTENTS

◤ FOREWORD

When I talked to my friend John Maxwell about the concept of this book, he told me that sometimes he has wrestled with keeping the changes he'd begun. I asked him if I could interview him and use our interchange as a foreword, and he graciously agreed.

Rob: A lot of books and talks focus on making changes, but very few address the importance of keeping those changes. What do you see as the difference between the two?

John: When I heard you talk about this concept, I immediately told you, "This needs to be in a book!" There is a fundamental difference between decision making and decision managing. We can make a choice in a moment, but we can forget it in the next moment. Success is found in managing that choice so it shapes a new trajectory for our lives. I've heard people say, "That decision changed my life," but that's not really the case. If the person's life was changed, it's because the person worked hard to implement the change over time—managed it—to create a new habit, a new pattern, a new way of living.

Rob: What are some of the changes you've tried hard to keep and manage?

John: I used to think that leaders liked change but many of their followers were resistant, but recently, I've learned that leaders are just as resistant . . . unless the change is their idea. When I was a young man, I met with Olan Hendricks. One day as we

had lunch together, he wrote on a napkin: "Growth = Change."
He explained, "You can make bad choices to change, and you'll
regress, but good choices are the essential building blocks of genuine growth. It's impossible to grow without making and keeping
positive changes.

The most difficult change for me was the point when I crossed
over from my role as a pastor to engage the business world. I was
already writing books, but they were for pastors. When I found
out that many people outside the church were buying and reading my books, I felt called to leave everything I knew, everything
that felt familiar and comfortable. This wasn't a tweak; it was a
massive change, and it took me about three years to incorporate
those changes into a new way of thinking, relating, writing, and
speaking. During that time, I talked to a lot of business leaders
and asked a lot of questions. All leadership principles come from
the Bible, but now I had to figure out how to communicate those
things in a way that believers and unbelievers could hear.

Rob: What are some mid-course corrections that have enabled you to keep the change?

John: We incorporate change much more readily during times
of adversity rather than times of unfettered success. Bill Gates
says that success is "a lousy teacher" because people think they
can't lose and they try to hold on to what they have. The greatest
detriment to tomorrow's success is today's success. People seldom change unless they have to, but too often, they wait too long.

One of the disciplines I live by is the understanding that I'm
continuously changing. I'm committed to keep growing, and that
always involves disruption, challenge, and change. I'm not surprised when I face setbacks, and I try to be honest about them.

It's important to be both bold and authentic—to constantly reach for more and admit the reality of the struggle.

Rob: What advice do you have for people who realize keeping the change is a marathon run instead of just a sprint?

John: Too many people have an arbitrary finish line for their life's race. When they get there, all their passion and energy quickly fade—they're still alive, but they've stopped growing, learning, and changing. That's very sad. It's most common for people who look to retirement as their finish line, but it can happen for younger people who have a vision of their dream job, the perfect spouse, or a desired lifestyle. Before that point, change has meaning, but after meeting that goal, change is inconvenient. I believe living outside our comfort zone is the right place to be. When I'm too comfortable, I know something's wrong: I'm beginning to lose my edge and avoiding change.

If you have only goals, when you meet them, you ask, "What's next?" But if you're committed to grow, you'll accomplish your goals, but you'll always be stretching yourself to learn more and be more . . . and you'll do whatever it takes to manage those decisions so you can keep the change. In other words, when we keep the change about one decision, we're primed to make and keep the next change in our expanding pattern of growth.

Years ago I spoke to about two thousand people at a leadership conference, and after one of my talks, a young man came up to me and said, "I've made a decision today. I want to do what you do."

I replied, "That wonderful, but to do what I do, you have to do what I did."

He looked a bit puzzled, so I explained, "You're looking at the finished product, but you don't see the days, months, and years of continuous challenge and change. If you're not willing to pay the price and do the did, you won't have the opportunity to do the do. The did always comes before the do. I hope he understood and followed my advice.

◢ INTRODUCTION:
WHAT'S THE DEAL?

In the early morning of December 11, 2014, I was working out in our basement. Later in the day, Becca, Connor, Logan, and I were going to take a flight to New York. We needed a family vacation, and this trip was going to be perfect. Like most things I get into, my workouts weren't relaxed and calm. I used a video curriculum called "Insanity," and the trainer pushed people to the limits. About twenty minutes into my workout, I was following his shouted directions when suddenly it felt like a spring snapped in my chest! I fell to the floor and wondered, *What in the world was that?*

Immediately, I had the sensation that I was on fire. Beads of sweat dripped from every part of me, and I instantly came to the conclusion: *I'm having a heat stroke.* I was sure it couldn't be a heart attack because I'd recently had a thorough physical at the Cooper Clinic in Dallas, and the doctors said my heart was in great shape.

I felt really bad, and the pain was getting worse. I began to wonder if I was going to die in the basement all alone. I forced myself to stand up and stagger up two flights of stairs to our bedroom where Becca was sleeping. It took everything in me to get there, and I collapsed on the floor. I moaned, "Becca, Becca."

She asked, "Where are you?"

I groaned, "I'm on the floor. Something's wrong." She jumped out of bed and knelt down. She saw that I was sweating profusely.

I told her, "I think I'm having a heat stroke. I can't stop sweating . . . and I felt something really strange in my chest."

She was alarmed and asked, "Should I call 9-1-1?"

I mumbled, "I don't know. Maybe this will pass." I glanced over to the bathroom. I was sure the tile floor would feel cool, so I crawled over and collapsed again on the floor. I had forgotten that our bathroom floor was heated in the winter. It was like lying on a hot stove! I crawled back to the bedroom and said, "Yeah, this is bad. You'd better make the call. I'll go to the front door to wait for the ambulance."

On my slow and unsteady stumble to the front door, I felt my jaw tightening and my left arm began to go numb. Then I threw up. I still wondered if this could be a heart attack. (Okay, I may be a little slow.) Becca stayed on the phone with the emergency operator, and when she described my symptoms, the operator told her to give me aspirin to chew and swallow immediately.

A few minutes later, the paramedics arrived. They came in with their bags and placed monitors on my chest. I must have mumbled that it could be a heart attack because it took only seconds for one of them to announce, "Oh yeah, you're having a heart attack."

As a pastor who has been at the bedside of dozens of people who have suffered heart attacks, you'd think I'd have more information about how they work. I didn't. I asked, "Are you going to give me a shot to fix it?"

To his credit, the paramedic didn't laugh out loud, but he left no room for doubt: "No, you're going in for surgery right now!"

The paramedic asked, "What hospital do you want us to take you to?"

I answered, "Where would you go?"

He said, "Abbot."

"Then take me there!" It wasn't the hospital closest to our house, but if that's the one the paramedics recommended, it sounded good to me.

As soon as they put me in the ambulance, I realized I'd missed the chance for some "last words" to Connor and Logan. I grabbed my phone and texted, "Take care of your mom. I love her. I've been faithful to her. I want you to find a wife like her. I love Jesus, and I want to see you in heaven. Serve Him forever." That's it. That's what I wanted to tell my sons if this was the last thing they heard or read from me.

A minute or two later, I wanted to ask the people in our church to pray for me, so I sent out this tweet:

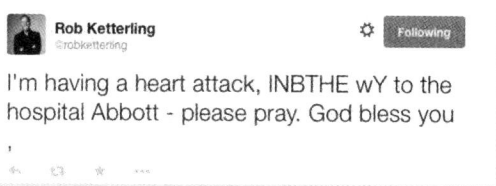

Rob Ketterling
@robketterling   ☆ Following

I'm having a heart attack, INBTHE wY to the hospital Abbott - please pray. God bless you

(I guess plenty of people wondered about the misspelling and awkward phrasing. I found out that a lot of them thought my Twitter account had been hacked!)

I thought Becca was in our car behind the ambulance. All the way to the hospital, I texted her, "I love you." "I'm so glad I married you." "You're the best. I love you so much." She was in the front seat of the ambulance.

The paramedic watched me send some texts and asked, "What are you doing?"

I said, "I'm telling people I love them. I don't want to leave anything unsaid."

She shook her head and almost barked, "You're not dying in *my* ambulance! I'm taking care of you!"

That was news to me. I asked, "Really?"

"Really!" she smiled. "You're not dying on my watch."

That was a huge relief. Actually, I wasn't sure she was telling me the truth. She might have wanted to sound optimistic so I wouldn't panic and make things worse, but I decided to trust her. (I found out later that one of the paramedics had a daughter who had started attending our church. She was getting an up close and personal look at her daughter's pastor in his moment of crisis.)

The ambulance sped through morning rush-hour traffic with the siren blaring. It would have been way better than a ride at Universal Studios, but I was a bit preoccupied. When we got to Abbot's ER, I was wheeled in through the double doors. Immediately, a doctor looked at the readings on the monitor and exclaimed for everyone around, "We've got a real one!" I thought that was a really strange thing to say. Then he looked at me and said, "You're having a heart attack right now. We're taking you into surgery."

As the nurses and physician's assistants prepped me for surgery, they began taking my shirt off. The EKG wires were tangled in my shirt, so they had some trouble getting it off. I must have been a little frustrated because I yelled, "Just cut it off! Let's go!" When they cut it off and threw it aside, I told them, "Save that shirt. It's going to be a sermon illustration."

One of the nurses leaned over and said, "We're going through a blood vessel in your groin, so we need to shave you there."

Immediately, I imagined one of them might be part of River Valley, so I insisted, "Only by someone who doesn't go to my church! If you shave your pastor's groin, you're never going to see him the same again."

Within minutes, the doctor found the blockages and inserted three stents. The nurse put a pressure wrap at the point of entry to stop the bleeding, and it was over.

That's "the rest of the story." I told the prequel in my book, *Change Before You Have To.* Here's a synopsis: Four years before that December day, Becca and I had dinner with some friends. We got caught up on our families and work, and then the conversation took an unexpected turn. I kidded my friend that he'd be lost without his wife around, and he responded, "You're no different! You're so high maintenance that you'd be lost without Becca!" I wish that had been the end of it, but I told him, "If I lost Becca, I'd have to lose some weight."

It doesn't take a genius to figure out how Becca would take this comment. My friend couldn't tolerate an ounce of ambiguity, so he chimed in and told Becca: "What Rob means is that if something happened to you and he had to go back on the market, he couldn't attract a woman like you looking fat like that."

I wanted to die, but first, I wanted to kill him! As it turned out, though, it was one of the most important moments in my life. I'd excused my indulgent eating habits for years, and I had the tonnage to prove it. I wasn't "pleasingly plump." I was fat, and it was time to do something about it: I made an appointment with my doctor and told him, "I want to get serious about this, so treat me like I just had a heart attack." I went on a diet and began to exercise. Gradually, the excess weight came off. Within a few months, I lost thirty pounds, and I looked and felt better than I had for years. My doctor was glad I was finally doing something about my weight and sky-high level of cholesterol. He told me, "If you'd kept going, you were a prime candidate for a heart attack." Fast forward four years to the day I had my heart attack, and the lesson is crystal clear: If I hadn't lost weight and gotten in better shape, there's a good chance my heart attack would have killed me. Five days into my hospital stay, the doctor showed me an image of my heart. In the previous four years of diet and exercise, my heart had developed new blood vessels called *collaterals*, a process commonly known as "natural bypasses," which provides blood flow outside the normal channels.[1]

I told the doctor, "A few years ago, I acted like I'd had a heart attack and made some dramatic changes. I changed before I had to, and it saved my life."[2]

During the first days in the hospital, the doctor warned me that the heart attack may have some long-term effects, and I may have to slow down, but thankfully, I regained 100 percent of my energy and drive. The event gave me a fresh sense of gratitude for the gift of every day. I told everyone who would listen (and some who didn't want to) about my heart attack. At a restaurant, the waiter asked what I wanted to order, and I told him, "I'm glad to order dinner because I had a heart attack and almost died. Being able to eat is such a blessing. Do you know Jesus?" Finally, after a year, Becca and the boys told me, "Enough about your heart attack!" Okay, okay, I got the message (but I'm still really grateful).

AFTER THE START

We need to find ways to keep moving in the new direction so the change becomes permanent.

The main point of my previous book is that we have a choice: we can wait for a crisis to force us to change, or we can have the wisdom to change before we have to. This book takes the principle a step further: I didn't just change before I had to; *I kept the change.* Quite often, we come to a crossroads and take a new path, but distractions and difficulties slow our progress . . . or bring us to a dead stop. It's not enough just to start well—though that's crucial—we need to find ways to keep moving in the new direction so the change becomes permanent. Far too often, our cost-benefit analysis is skewed in the wrong direction. We look at the price we have to pay to keep a needed change, and we bail out. Instead, we need to focus on the benefits and let that reality fuel our engines. After my embarrassing dinner conversation, I was committed to lose weight, and the results were better than I imagined: I had so much more energy, my mind was sharper in meetings and conversations, my clothes fit better, I could look at myself in the mirror without flinching, I earned Becca's respect, and strangely, I enjoyed eating even more than before. Food tasted better because I was more careful to choose what I really like.

When I was overweight, I found ways to diffuse the shame. I carried my weight in my gut, so, because I'm a pastor, I called by bulging middle a "pulpit blister" and insisted "there, ...ore of me to love." Humor was my way to avoid the painful (and bloated) reality ... but no longer. No more denial, no more excuses, no more trying to hide something everyone could plainly see.

I get it. Change is hard. We live in an instant society, and we expect results with only a quick search and a couple of clicks. We have online banking, drive-thru restaurants, same-day delivery, streaming movies, and microwaved meals. I'm not advocating that we go back to the Stone Age, but it would be a good idea to have a more realistic grasp of how change is initiated and established. Most of us start with deficit thinking: we've been doing the same things for so long that change seems like a mountain too big to climb. It's too hard, it takes too long, and it's just not worth it. When we come to this conclusion, we're defeated before the game even starts. I've heard people explain that their bad habit is a generational curse: "My grandfather was like this, my father was like this, and I'm stuck in this too. This rut is my destiny, and it'll never change."

Over many years of talking with people about the need to make and keep changes, I've noticed three distinct groups:

> Some have given up before they ever started. They live without hope, drive, or purpose.

> Many have tried to change and have made some good-faith attempts, but it hasn't lasted. They're frustrated, but open to getting some help.

> And a few grasp the principles of keeping the change. They live in the powerful confluence of vitality, hope, and gratitude.

This book is about helping the first two groups join the third one.

If lasting change has been elusive, you're not alone. An article in *Business Insider* cites a company survey of 1,000 employees who invested in personal development courses and worked toward their goals for 90 days. The data showed that 96 percent of their efforts completely failed. The author joked, "I'm opening a gym called Resolutions. It will have exercise equipment in it for the first two weeks and then it turns into a bar for the remainder of the year." The buzz of a motivational environment and the big commitment wear off pretty quickly if we don't construct an environment of personal encouragement, reasonable schedules, and good resources to keep us on track.[3]

In a *Forbes* article about the reasons business transformations often fail, Brent Gleason lists many contributing issues, but the chief cause is "change battle fatigue." The principle applies to individuals, families, businesses, churches, and every other organization. Past failures, a cloudy vision, lack of support, and insufficient resources erode enthusiasm and derail commitment. Gleason explains,

It's awfully hard for managers and staff to get motivated when they believe that the latest project from on high is going to die just like the last one—no matter what they do. Fear makes change intensely personal. People fear for their income. They worry about their families. They wonder what will happen to their careers. When people are afraid, they literally can't hear or think as well. It's much harder for them to take in important information when their minds are reeling. This can be a big distraction that undermines your team's ability to focus and stay productive . . . just when you need them most.[4]

MY PROMISE

Fear . . . worry . . . doubt . . . a sense of hopelessness. These are very real hindrances to change that lasts and makes a difference. My promise is that if you'll dig deep enough to focus on the benefits instead of making excuses, amazing things will happen. You'll get out of the rut you've endured far too long, frustration will be transformed into confidence, and embarrassment will be changed into joy. In this book, you'll be inspired and challenged, but you'll also be equipped to make change take root and grow. I like to think about skilled craftsmen who use "cheats" to accomplish something that seems impossible to others. For instance, I'm not a woodworker, but I love to watch a cabinet or furniture maker use a special technique to join two pieces of wood or turn a corner or put inlays into a tabletop. (Here's looking at you, *This Old House!*) I want to give you some cheats that make it easier to keep the change. Some will be very obvious, but others will probably be new to you. I can always tell a point has penetrated deep into my soul when I want to shout, "Why didn't I see this before?" I hope you have a lot of those moments as you read these chapters.

You'll get out of the rut you've endured far too long, frustration will be transformed into confidence, and embarrassment will be changed into joy.

In the Bible, the apostle Paul wrote his letter to the Philippians as a thank-you note because they had supported him in his outreach across the Roman Empire. In one of the more memorable parts of the letter, he explains that we may have many different pursuits, but one is far more important than all the rest: "Yes, everything else is worthless when compared with the infinite value of knowing Christ Jesus my Lord. For his sake I have discarded everything else, counting it all as garbage, so that I could gain Christ and become one with him."

But Paul knew that change is hard, and keeping change requires us to look back at how far we've come as well as looking ahead to where God wants us to go. He pointed to the future:

> I focus on this one thing: Forgetting the past and looking forward to what lies ahead, I press on to reach the end of the race and receive the heavenly prize for which God, through Christ Jesus, is calling us. Let all who are spiritually mature agree on these things. If you disagree on some point, I believe God will make it plain to you. But we must hold on to the progress we have already made. (Philippians 3:8-9, 13-16)

Have you had trouble keeping change that's important to you? Of course you have. We all have. It may be in your handling of money, your relationships with your spouse and children, your weight and physical conditioning, or a habit you've tried to break. To keep the change, the first step is to rearrange your agenda so that Christ is your treasure of "infinite value," and the second step is to "hold on to the progress we have already made."

At the end of this introduction and each chapter, you'll find some questions to stimulate your thinking, promote good discussions, and prompt targeted prayers. These aren't timed tests, so you don't get extra credit for rushing through them. Take your time, consider the principles and how to apply them, and take the steps God leads you to take.

CONSIDER THIS:

1. What might be some reasons people have trouble keeping an important change?

2. In what area of your life has keeping change proven to be difficult? What have been some of the distractions and discouragements?

3. What will be some of the benefits of keeping the change?

4. Look again at the passage from Philippians at the end of the Introduction. What are Paul's directives? And what are the motivations he cites?

5. What do you hope to get out of this book?

CHAPTER 1

◢ PROMISING STARTS

Nothing paralyzes our lives like the attitude that things can never change. We need to remind ourselves that God can change things. Outlook determines outcome. If we see only the problems, we will be defeated; but if we see the possibilities in the problems, we can have victory.

—Warren Wiersbe

B efore the double date that shined a spotlight on my weight problem, I'd tried diets . . . lots of diets. I often looked at myself in the mirror and concluded, *I really should do something about my gut.* I promised myself that I'd start the very next Monday . . . or the first of the next month . . . or the first of the next year. The prompts were many and varied: my shirts were too tight, somebody teased me about being so fat, and my back hurt so bad that I couldn't swing a golf club without pain. I actually changed my swing to lower the level of pain. Moe Norman teaches "natural golf," which involves a motion that uses your weight for power without twisting your body like a normal golf swing. It looks weird, but it didn't hurt my back. People I didn't know saw my swing and I could almost hear them laughing, and my friends asked, "What in the world are you doing?" I could have just lost weight and gotten in shape, but instead, I changed my golf game to compensate for being overweight and out of shape. Smart, huh?

When I was overweight, I developed a hawk-eye to notice people who had (let me put it this way) more bulk than me. Then I could say, "Well, at least I'm not *that* fat!" And from time to time, I had to change my entire wardrobe to buy pants and shirts that would fit over my increasing girth.

I tried all kinds of diets, from Atkins to Weight Watchers to Nutrisystem to others I found online. I bought prepackaged meals to be sure I (and our whole family) stayed on the diets. Our freezer was crammed full of dinners we never ate . . . because I soon gave up on one diet and launched into another one that promised quicker results. I knew I didn't really want to go on a diet, so I figured that spending a lot of money on a plan would motivate me to stay on it. What a waste . . .

Every diet and exercise plan was a hundred-yard dash. I was absolutely, totally, radically committed . . . for a brief moment. I can't count how many times I felt so good about myself because I had a protein bar for breakfast, a salad for lunch, and small portions for dinner, just like the infomercials tell you to do. I wanted to shout, "Look at me! I'm doing the diet thing, and I'm winning!" But after a few days, I got on the scales and watched the digital numbers climb to my weight before I started the diet. I was so disappointed: "I did all this for nothing!" (If you've been successful in dieting, don't send me any angry emails or tweets. I get it: Diets work *if you stick with them!*)

But my sprints weren't just in diets. I bought multiple treadmills, a stair stepper, weights, and other devices, and one day I found the hope of the future on an infomercial: an ab cruncher! The guy on television looked super fit. He got into the device on the floor and pulled his head and torso up again and again. It was perfect for my gut. I was going to do what the infomercial said: I'd "rock my way to rock hard abs!" It looked so easy, and that guy looked so good! This was going to be the key, the solution I'd been looking for. I used it for about three days. When I didn't lose five pounds in those three days, I gave up on it. (Actually, I bought another one a few months later—a newer model that promised even better results. I used it for four days. Is that progress?)

The payoffs for my efforts weren't good enough to keep me going. It didn't take Becca long to realize my bursts of enthusiasm weren't going to stand the test of time. The evidence was obvious—I had a basement full of gadgets that were taking up space and collecting dust. After the fourth or fifth aborted launch, Becca rolled her eyes every time I told her about a new diet and exercise plan. Sometimes she just looked at me and said, "You're busted. You're not going to follow through with it. Go ahead and eat another dessert." (I wanted to say, "Hey, I thought you were on my side!")

Misguided expectations are common in every kind of change. I've talked to men who have come with their wives to marriage counseling, and some of them have made solemn commitments to change. They put the clamps on their explosive anger for one day, and they expected their wives to suddenly and completely forget all the pain they've felt for the seven years of their relationship. They come back and complain, "I did what you told me to do, but it didn't work. She *still* doesn't trust me."

I ask her, "How long did he last between blow-ups?"

"About twelve hours."

I turn to him and explain, "For seven years your wife has seen that your anger is out of control and she can't trust you to be calm and reasonable when you disagree with her. The damage has been going on for a long time, and the wound is deep. It's going to take at least seven months of self-control for her to trust you . . . and with every new explosion, you're starting over."

I'm sorry to say that a lot of guys bail out at that point. They can't imagine being reasonable for more than a day.

A recent study showed that 38 percent of Americans made New Year's resolutions, but 80 percent of them had given up by the first of February.[5] Starting isn't the problem; keeping the change is far more challenging.

Starting isn't the problem; keeping the change is far more challenging.

Every attempt to make a change, no matter how it turns out, demonstrates faith, hope, and courage . . . and I applaud that! In fact, if people have lost the hope and energy to even give change a try, they're in big trouble. As you can tell, I'm the very last person to criticize anyone for trying and failing!

Sometimes our expectations are just too high. For instance, I've talked to people who made a commitment to read the Bible every day, and when they miss a day or two, they get discouraged and quit. I tell them, "No problem. God didn't go anywhere during the days you missed. Just start again. And if you miss again, start again." The point is the same in our commitment to get out of debt, spend time with our kids, go to bed earlier, avoid too much time with negative people who bring us down, eat smaller portions, exercise, and dozens of other habits we want to change. We need a healthy blend of ruthlessness and realism. We need to be dedicated to the goal and the process, but we also need to realize we're going to mess up from time to time. When that happens, we don't make excuses; instead, we admit the failure and start again.

Alcoholics and addicts of all kinds know that a single slip can push them over the edge and back into their destructive habits. They need to be especially diligent to watch for triggers, and they use the acronym HALT to remind them to be careful whenever they feel Hungry, Angry, Lonely, or Tired. In the first days, weeks, and months of being clean and sober, relapse is constantly lurking around the corner. If it happens—or *when* it happens—it's not time to give up. It's time to be more determined to be around people in recovery who are making good decisions, eliminate or minimize triggers, and trust God for hope and strength.

ANGER: ROCKET FUEL OF CHANGE

In bigger issues of abuse and justice, our motivations will be deeper and stronger. Not long after George Floyd was killed on the street in Minneapolis in May of 2020, I was asked to speak to a gathering of national and local leaders, including some from the NAACP. As you recall, this incident enflamed racial tension throughout the country. On one side, marches decrying violence were held in cities and towns throughout the nation and even in cities across the world. And on the other side, people were careful to say that the officer who knelt on Floyd's neck for nine minutes doesn't represent the vast majority of police officers in our communities.

Anger was a very present emotion in countless hearts, and I wanted to acknowledge that fact. I told the gathering, "I still think there's hope for America to resolve our racial struggles, and here's why: our anger shows that we believe things should be different, things should be better, things should be resolved so people respect each other. Our anger demonstrates that we haven't given up. We haven't shrugged our shoulders and moaned, 'That's just the way it is, and that's just the way it's always going to be.'" I explained, "When couples come to me for marriage counseling and I see the fury on their faces and hear their harsh words, there's hope for them because their emotion shows they still care about their relationship. But when couples walk through my door with blank stares and apathetic, stone-cold responses, I have very little hope for reconciling their marriage. They're done. Game over." I concluded my talk by saying, "I believe there's hope for black America and white America to be healed because our anger shows we still care. This raw emotion shows we still believe things can and should be better, and we're committed to find a way through to understanding, respect, and love for each other."

In the same way, people who have been sexually, physically, or verbally abused need to tap into their anger to confront the abuser, loving him or her enough to challenge the sin, and depending on the response, offer a path to reconciliation. (God calls us to forgive whether the other person repents or not, but reconciliation requires much more than a quick "I'm sorry" from the offender. Trust can only be rebuilt through a process.) Prolonged abuse and neglect are some of the most painful and difficult situations to change, and there's very little hope of substantive change without the fuel of righteous anger.

John Chrysostom, an early church father, commented, "He who does not get angry, when there is just cause for being so, commits sin. For unreasonable patience [that is, refusing to be angry when it's appropriate] is the hotbed of many vices; it fosters negligence and incites not only the wicked but the good to do wrong."[6] That's exactly what I've seen in the lives of people who have become passive as a way to cope with pain inflicted by someone who should care for them. It gives permission to the abuser, and it causes the victim to avoid speaking the truth in love.

(By the way, in this book I'm addressing the full range of changes, from relatively minor to monumental. As we take steps to grow and become "mature in the Lord, measuring up to the full and complete standard of Christ" (Ephesians 4:13), some of us need to tweak our schedules and priorities, but others need to make more radical changes that will shake the foundations of their lives—finally facing deep hurts caused by people who should have provided love and safety, and addressing all the promising but self-defeating ways they've tried to cope with the pain. And of course, some who are reading the book are the ones who caused this pain. You'll find a number of principles and illustrations for the monumental changes. If the people who are keeping these changes can take courageous steps, the rest of you can, too.)

Far too many Christians believe all anger is sinful and wrong, but the Apostle Paul commands us: "In your anger do not sin" (Ephesians 4:26 NIV). This means that if we get angry just to defend our fragile egos and control people, that's sin. But when there is injustice or another valid cause for anger, and we don't get angry, that's also sin. To paraphrase one of the early church leaders: "If we don't get angry when there is just cause for it, our lack of anger demonstrates a lack of compassion for the one who is wounded. Unreasonable patience creates many problems, giving a green light to wicked people and causing good people to close their eyes to injustice."[7] In very painful relationships, victims of abuse or abandonment often shut down emotionally to avoid becoming the target of more wrath. Change, growth, healing, forgiveness—and the chance for reconciliation—only happen if they're angry enough to stand up and say, "No more! Let's find a better way to relate to each other."

And sometimes, it's good and right for us to be the recipients of another person's anger. That, too, is a fuel for change. When someone speaks up and speaks out to challenge us, we have an opportunity to take the blinders off and see how we're affecting people . . . quite often, the people we love. Jesus gave the religious leaders chances to change when He called them on their hypocrisy. They didn't just call people to follow the Old Testament law; they multiplied so many more laws, rules, and regulations that the people felt overwhelmed with guilt instead of loving and following God with full hearts. Jesus didn't mince words. He told them,

> "You hypocrites! Isaiah was right when he prophesied
>   about you, for he wrote,
> 'These people honor me with their lips,
>   but their hearts are far from me.
> Their worship is a farce,
>   for they teach man-made ideas as commands from
>   God.'" (Matthew 15:7-9)

And the Apostle Paul wasn't shy about speaking the truth. When the new believers in Galatia drifted away from the freedom, love, and power of the gospel after religious leaders came from Jerusalem and taught them they had to add keeping the law to God's grace, Paul called them on the carpet:

Oh, foolish Galatians! Who has cast an evil spell on you? For the meaning of Jesus Christ's death was made as clear to you as if you had seen a picture of his death on the cross. Let me ask you this one question: Did you receive the Holy Spirit by obeying the law of Moses? Of course not! You received the Spirit because you believed the message you heard about Christ. How foolish can you be? After starting your new lives in the Spirit, why are you now trying to become perfect by your own human effort? Have you experienced so much for nothing? Surely it was not in vain, was it? (Galatians 3:1-4)

Over the top? No, right on target. Righteous anger is a powerful motivation to change—for us and for the people we love—but we need to be careful that we're not just venting our rage to intimidate people and get our way. Righteous anger is a form of love, not hate; it seeks to build up, not tear down; it offers a path to reconciliation, not division. Don't rush by that sentence too quickly. In fact, read it again. There's no question that anger is like gasoline: it can either power our engines for positive change, or it can cause all kinds of damage. Most of us aren't exactly experts at righteous anger! We need some help from mature, wise people who can show us how to harness its power.

Righteous anger is a form of love, not hate; it seeks to build up, not tear down; it offers a path to reconciliation, not division.

More broadly, when we look at change that needs to happen in our lives, we need enough internal fire that says: "No more! This has to change!" The powerful emotion propels us to make and keep changes in how we handle our money, how we relate to our families, and any other habit that requires a do-over.

THE POWER OF STORIES

We live in a "celebrity culture." We're bombarded with images and stories of film stars, great athletes, business moguls, and people who are famous just for being famous. When we hear them talk about changes in their lives, it's often about ditching a lover or a spouse for an upgrade, buying a bigger yacht, receiving an award, or earning a bigger contract. We may be enamored with them because the media has put them in front of us 24/7, but I'm far more inspired by regular people who have found the courage to make promising starts in the long process of change. Here are a few that rev my engines:

Jaime, a young woman who escaped a toxic marriage, brought her young son to one of our church campuses in an attempt to find hope and healing for her devastated heart. She found Jesus as her Savior and Lord, and she got involved with some supportive women who poured themselves into her. She was so grateful for the love she received that she dedicated her life to help other women experience the wonder of grace in a community of strong, loving women. She was unwilling for her life to be defined by her painful past.

When Bryant was a boy, he had a rough time. Both of his parents were alcoholics, so he grew up with some deep hurts and big relational deficits. After leaving his parents' home and finding another place to live, his roommates invited him to come to church, where he heard the message of grace. Bryant used to know God, but the pain of his past got him off the right path. When he heard about God's amazing love and forgiveness, he thought it must be too good to be true, so he asked one of our pastors a pointed question: "Are you *sure* that Jesus forgives sins?" The pastor assured him that Jesus forgives every sin. Bryant paused, and then he began listing some: "Would Jesus forgive this one?" The pastor nodded. "But would he forgive this one [which was a little bit bigger]?" He was assured again. "What about this one?"

"Yes, Jesus forgives that."

"Yeah, but what about this one?"

"That, too."

Finally, Bryant went for the big one: "What if someone killed somebody?"

The pastor assumed this was a hypothetical question, but Bryant wanted to see how far the forgiveness of Jesus would extend. Again, the pastor told him, "Yes, Jesus will forgive even a Mafia hitman who trusts in Him."

Bryant couldn't pass up the opportunity for Jesus to cleanse him and make him new, so he trusted in Christ, joined the church, got a job, and saw his life turned around. Eventually, he met Sarah, a lovely woman, and the two of them got married. Today, he's a leader in our church, a trophy of God's amazing love and power. Every time I see him, he gives me a huge hug and tells me how grateful he is for the people of our church.

Daralee is a young woman who got pregnant unexpectedly. When her boyfriend heard the news, he abandoned her, and her own family strongly encouraged her to have an abortion. Unexpectedly, her boyfriend's mother told her, "If you follow through with the abortion because of all the pressure and because you feel alone, I promise that you'll regret it for the rest of your life. Don't make this decision out of fear. You aren't alone. I'll be with you the whole way." After Daralee had her baby, she met a young man named Pat, who was a single father. They fell in love, found new hope in Jesus, got married, and today are a beacon of hope for those around them.

Brad's life was devastated by the pressures and losses he suffered during Covid. He had completely lost hope, but he came to our church, met Christ as his Savior, and found a new trajectory of meaning and purpose. He's serving people, loving them the way Jesus loves him. Like Bryant, when I see Brad, he gives me a bear hug as he wipes away tears of gratitude and joy.

In 2014, Derek was admitted to the ER for a drug overdose. In fact, he woke up in the hospital not knowing how he got there. One of our pastors visited him and gave him my first book, *Change Before You Have To*. He didn't think he was interested, but he had nothing else to do, so he read it. He surrendered to God the wreckage he had created, and Jesus transformed his life. Today, he is the Lead Facilities Manager at our church, and he still smiles when we talk about the remarkable changes in his life. Everyone can see it! (When I asked him for permission to use his story, he commented how incredible it is that his story is now being shared in the sequel of the book that changed his life. *That's keeping the change!*)

As a young woman, Mona ran away from God. Her best friend was a drug dealer, and she began using cocaine and other drugs to numb her pain. One day, she took a step back to look at her life, and she told herself, *I can't live this way anymore!* She found Jesus, and today she's my executive assistant. She's the sweetest, most responsible person I've ever known. It's unfathomable to me to think that she had been an addict so far from God.

Now, let me share a story that's really close to home . . . because it was actually *in our home.* When I was four years old, my mom and dad asked my brother Rick and me if we'd be willing for them to become foster parents. They asked, "Would you be willing to share your mom and dad with other children who don't have places to live? Our home would become their home, at least for a while."

Rick and I had no clue what they were really asking, so we said, "Sure! That would be great!"

Over the next twenty years, about 100 girls lived in our home, from two to seven at a time. My dad put up bunk beds in our family room. (We had only two bathrooms, so showers were strictly limited to five minutes, max.) Some of the girls were with us for only a day, but others stayed for years. I remember one of them became so close to my parents that she asked my dad to walk her down the aisle when she got married.

When I was old enough to notice what was going on in our home, I saw that all of the girls had the privilege to live, at least for a while, in a loving, healthy environment, but their responses varied widely. For some, my parents' love didn't penetrate their powerful (and totally understandable) defenses, and change didn't happen at all. Some changed while they were with us, but when they left, they reverted to lifestyles and relationships that opened old wounds and caused more heartache. And thankfully, the love took root in the hearts of some of those girls, and their lives were transformed by their time under our roof. Their lives are testimonies of God's life-changing love, and it's a testimony of God using my mom and dad to create a loving, stable home for them. I believe that even those whose change didn't last at least have a memory of grace and kindness that may someday bring them back to God and a more sustainable, healthy change.

One of the girls has grown up and now attends our church. The impact of my parents was so strong that she has recreated a new legacy of love for her own children and grandchildren. Yes, grandchildren. Her time in our home happened a long, long time ago, and God is still using my mom and dad's influence in her life.

As you've been reading this chapter and an emotion has bubbled up in your heart, that's a great sign! Even if it's anger or sadness or fear, begin to face it. Those painful feelings may have caused you to run from change because you didn't want to uncover all the pain and loss, but now God can use them to propel you to make the changes you know you need to make. Stay in that emotion. Let it give you a fierce resolve to say "No!" to what has been and say "Yes!" to a better future.

Let me put it this way: If you're reading this book, there's hope for you. If you've read this far, there's hope for you. If you're going to turn the page and read the next chapter, there's hope for you. That's a promising start!

We cannot change our past. We cannot change the fact that people act in a certain way. We cannot change the inevitable. The only thing we can do is play on the one string we have, and that is our attitude.

—*Chuck Swindoll*

CONSIDER THIS:

1. What might be some of the reasons 80 percent of people who have good intentions and set New Year's resolutions fail by the first of February? Which of these is a reason you've used to bail out on change you've committed to?

2. Has your commitment to change been more like a hundred-yard dash or a marathon? Explain your answer.

3. Look back at Ephesians 4:26. A lot of people assume anger is always wrong. How would you help them see that the feeling of anger is neutral, but the actions of anger can be either productive or destructive?

4. In what ways is anger an essential fuel for change? How do other emotions (such as fear, shame, hurt, or even gratitude) affect our motivations to change?

5. Think back over the last couple of years. What are some promising starts you've made to change? What do those starts say about your level of hope that life can be better?

CHAPTER 2

◢ RECOGNIZE THE SLIDE

Complacency is the last hurdle standing between any team and its potential greatness.

—*Pat Riley, legendary NBA coach*

It's so easy. So incredibly easy. No matter how fired up I am about turning a corner and going in a new direction, opportunities to bail out seem to come fast and furiously. And again, I'm not alone. In one way, the Bible is a chronicle of people who were given golden opportunities but found creative ways to mess things up. Think of Adam and Eve, Jacob, Moses, and most of the kings of Israel . . . and then think of Peter—we don't need a better example in the New Testament than him! But I want focus on a man who had everything going for him, but repeatedly blew it. It was the first king of Israel, a man named Saul.

At the end of the period of the judges, God's people got tired of looking around at other nations and seeing them with kings to lead them. They didn't want to trust God to lead them; they wanted their own king. The last judge, Samuel, asked God what He wanted to do, and God said, "I'll give them what they want, but they'll be sorry!" . . . or words to that effect. God led Samuel to a man who was part Paul Rudd and part Dwayne "The Rock" Johnson—Saul was the tallest, most handsome man in the land. And he was rich. His physical attributes commanded attention, and his status earned respect. Let's take a quick glance at the ways Saul blew it:

> When Samuel anointed Saul as the king, God's Spirit was poured out on him, and he prophesied among the prophets. It was a sure sign that God was with him, but immediately, when Saul's uncle asked him where he'd been, Saul was too afraid to tell him that he was the first king of Israel (1 Samuel 10:1-16).

> Samuel called all the people together to introduce King Saul, but like a comedy, when he turned to make the grand announcement ("And . . . here he is!") Saul wasn't there! The Israelites looked for him, and they finally found him hiding among the baggage. Before he even started, he doubted himself and God (1 Samuel 10:17-24).

> When the Philistines came to fight against Saul's army, Samuel directed Saul to wait for him to come with instructions from the Lord. But as the days passed, Saul grew impatient and took matters into his own hands. He offered a sacrifice to God instead of waiting for Samuel to offer it. When Samuel arrived, he told Saul that this was a costly mistake. Samuel rebuked him: "Listen! Obedience is better than sacrifice, and submission is better than offering the fat of rams" (1 Samuel 15:22).

> The next one is, in my opinion, the most boneheaded blunder Saul made—it involved his son, Jonathan. When battle with the Philistines was imminent, Saul was in big trouble. Many of his men had fled, and the Philistine army was strong.

Saul's army of 600 had only farm implements: plows, mattocks, axes, and sickles. In the face of this hopeless situation, Jonathan showed incredible courage. He and his armor-bearer attacked a Philistine outpost, and the attack was so successful that the Philistines panicked and ran. God caused an earthquake to add to the chaos, and the soldiers who had abandoned Saul's army came back to fight at Jonathan's side. But that's not the end of the story. In Saul's excitement, he impulsively vowed that any of his soldiers who ate anything before the victory was complete would be executed. But . . . there was a little problem: Jonathan wasn't there to hear the order, and he ate some honey to strengthen himself as he raced after the enemy. How would Saul respond? Get this: this young man had saved his father and his father's kingdom, and his dad decided it was more important to fulfill his vow than to honor his son for his courage. In front of everyone, he told Jonathan, "You shall surely die." The people were so outraged that they stopped Saul. How much respect do you think they had for him then? (1 Samuel 14:1-45) (And what do you think the conversation around the table was like that night at Saul's house?)

> In the next scene, God gave Saul clear instructions about defeating several allied armies, but Saul disobeyed. When Samuel called him on it, he made excuses and blamed his soldiers. That was the last straw. God told Samuel He would anoint another king to take Saul's place (1 Samuel 15:1-26).

> You may be familiar with the story of David coming to the soldiers' camp to bring bread and cheese to his brothers, and there, he saved Saul's bacon by killing the menacing giant

Goliath. You'd think Saul would be grateful, but soon after that, as David played soothing music to calm Saul's troubled heart, Saul tried to skewer David with a spear! (1 Samuel 18:6-11)

> David, the nation's hero, became a refugee. He gathered a rag-tag group of outsiders, and together, they formed a special ops force. They ran from Saul's army, fought the Philistines, and found a way to stay alive. Finally, as the battle went against him, Saul asked his armorbearer to end his life. King Saul died, along with David's best friend Jonathan, and David became the new king (1 Samuel 31:1-6).

When we look at this sad saga, we notice that Saul tried to cover up his cowardice, disobedience, and treachery with a long list of excuses.

Things could have gone very differently for Saul, but time after time, he slid down the slope of self-deception and excuses. When we look at this sad saga, we notice that Saul tried to cover up his cowardice, disobedience, and treachery with a long list of excuses. At each point, though, he was sure he was doing exactly the right thing. In *Leadership and Self-Deception*, the author explains:

Self-deception is like this. It blinds us to the true causes of problems, and once we're blind, all the "solutions" we can think of will actually make matters worse. Whether at work or at home, self-deception obscures the truth about ourselves, corrupts our view of others and our circumstances, and inhibits our ability to make wise and helpful decisions.[8]

That's what happened to Saul, and that's what happens to us when we take the convenient route of self-deception instead of opening our eyes, seeing reality, and making wise, courageous choices.

EXCUSES, EXCUSES

It's easy to slide back into our old ways. Too easy. Let's look at some common elements of self-deception and the excuses that make perfect sense.

Faulty memory

One of the most common reasons people don't translate good intentions and a good start into lasting change is memory loss. No, I don't mean that kind of memory loss! They make a little progress, but they're discouraged by how far they still need to go. They forget the heartache, dysfunction, and strained relationships they suffered before they began the process. Remembering where we've come from is essential . . . just like it's important in our testimonies to recount our condition before we trusted Christ. Moses warned the people (and us), "Only be careful, and watch yourselves closely so that you do not forget the things your eyes have seen or let them fade from your heart as long as you

live. Teach them to your children and to their children after them"
(Deuteronomy 4:9 NIV).

The Samson Syndrome

Samson was an expert at rationalizing. His birth was sur-
rounded by the presence of God, and undoubtedly, his parents
told him how special he was. In fact, he was one of the judges of
Israel. But as a young man, Samson had his eye on a Philistine
woman, and he married her. At the wedding feast, he tried to
impress the Philistines with a riddle about a lion he had recently killed with his bare hands. He gave them seven days to give
the answer, but they had no clue. On the last day, his new wife
wept and pleaded with him to tell her. He gave in, and she told
her Philistine friends. He was so angry that he returned home,
and his wife was given to his best man. Time after time, Samson
fought against the Philistines, but he continued to make friends
with them, and he baited them into contests of strength. He wanted to see how close he could come to disaster and still escape. It
was an adrenaline rush.

But eventually, his new girlfriend Delilah made a deal with
the Philistine leaders to expose the source of his strength. She
begged and pleaded until she wore him down, and he finally told
her: it was his hair. She conspired to have someone come into
their bedroom and cut his hair while he was asleep, and the next
morning, Samson was doomed: "Then she called, 'Samson, the
Philistines are upon you!' He awoke from his sleep and thought,
'I'll go out as before and shake myself free.' But he did not know
that the Lord had left him" (Judges 16:20 NIV).

The story of Samson shows that he violated his vow to honor
God over and over again. He had tried to fly close to the fire, and

he got burned. All along the way, he thought he had everything under control, but it was a delusion.

We may try to convince ourselves that our spending, our family time, our health, and our diversions are under control, but in reality, our excuses are leading us on a path to destruction. We say to ourselves, *I'll buy my kids something nice so they'll know I still love them.* Or, *It doesn't matter that my new laptop doesn't have a porn filter. I'm good.* Or, *I'll take my wife out to a nice dinner to make up for not being around.* I heard a speaker say, "An inch to the devil is an inch too much, 'cause he'll inch you and inch you 'til he's got you in his clutch." Paul put it this way, "So, if you think you are standing firm, be careful that you don't fall!" (1 Corinthians 10:12 NIV)

Not My Fault

Blame-shifting should be an Olympic sport because so many of us are pros at it! The first human, Adam, set the gold-medal standard. When God confronted him for eating the forbidden fruit, Adam told Him (presumably with a straight face), "It was the woman you gave me who gave me the fruit, and I ate it" (Genesis 3:12). This was a two-fer: Adam blamed Eve, and he blamed God for bringing Eve to him.

A spouse might say, "I wouldn't have had the affair if you weren't such a nag (or a bully)!" Or "I wouldn't be so angry if you were more responsible!" Or "If you made more money (or were more present with me and the kids), I wouldn't be so upset all the time." The examples are endless. Blame-shifting is a way of using harsh, condemning words to have power over another person . . . and wherever there are "blame throwers," there are always "blame sponges" who are willing to take the heat to avoid a bigger blowup. They've been told everything is their fault so long and so often that they believe it. This shatters their sense of self-confidence, so they're afraid to make even the simplest decisions. They don't feel safe talking openly about how they feel, so the resentment and emotional distance grow.

Just This Once

This is one of the most common misconceptions. We excuse ourselves by thinking, *I'll just buy this one expensive thing. I'll never need another one.* Or, *I'll watch this video just this once. It won't become a habit.* Or, *I'll blow up and scream at the kids just this once. They deserve it, and besides, they'll get over it.* This is a big enough problem with "minor" slips, but it's a calamity when that "one time" is an affair, a hit of a drug for a recovering addict, stealing from the company, or something else catastrophic. The truth is that a single step charts a new direction that may become a new normal, and tragically, some "once moments" lead to a lifetime of regrets.

Even as one foolish action requires a reversal, one positive step often sets a new direction. I once talked to a bill collector who contacts people who owe tens of thousands of dollars. When he asks how much they can pay right away, they often say, "Nothing. I'm broke." He developed a strategy to ask, "Can you pay $10?" The person often responds, "Yeah, I can pay that." He gives them an account so they can send money immediately from their phone, and he tells them, "Transfer $10 to this account." No delay, no excuses. He explained to me that if someone will do something even this small to change the direction from running from the debt to begin paying it down, they often stick with a payment plan and become debt free. Having them take the extra step to wire the money solidifies the commitment in their minds. "Just this once" can get us into big trouble, but "just this once" can also chart a new and better direction.

Solomon used an intriguing metaphor to describe how seemingly small indiscretions can have tragic consequences. He wrote, "Catch all the foxes, those little foxes, before they ruin the vineyard of love, for the grapevines are blossoming!" (Song of Solomon 2:15) Foxes are nocturnal and sneaky. Farmers seldom see them, but they see the damage they've caused. Solomon is warning us that even little foxes can cause great loss, just as seemingly little slides can inflict a lot of pain . . . for us and for those around us.

When people rent a storage facility, they don't use a frontend loader to fill it up. They take box after box. Jesus used this idea of incremental storage in His most famous sermon. He told the people who were on the hillside, "Don't store up treasures here on earth, where moths eat them and rust destroys them, and where thieves break in and steal. Store your treasures in heaven, where moths and rust cannot destroy, and thieves do not break in and steal. Wherever your treasure is, there the desires of your heart will also be" (Matthew 6:19-21). Every box is important. Where will we put the next one?

No One Can See

You've probably heard people in recovery say, "We're only as sick as our secrets." That painful truth applies to all of us, not just alcoholics and addicts. We become experts at shading the truth to disguise what we're doing. We tell ourselves, *Hey, it isn't hurting anybody.* But our secrets and lies inevitably create strains in the fabric of our relationships. Even if the other person doesn't know we're hiding the truth, we know, so we spend an inordinate amount of time and energy avoiding exposure. A single secret soon multiplies, and lying becomes our go-to strategy in relationships. Popular psychologist Brené Brown says that secrets and shame go hand-in-hand: "Shame loves secrecy. The most dangerous thing to do after a shaming experience is hide or bury our story. When we bury our story, the shame metastasizes. . . . If you put shame in a petri dish, it needs three ingredients to grow exponentially: secrecy, silence, and judgment. If you put the same amount of shame in the petri dish and douse it with empathy, it can't survive."[9]

We need to remember that we may be able to hide our behavior from people, but God sees it all. With equal assurance and warning, Solomon reminds us, "The Lord is watching everywhere, keeping his eye on both the evil and the good" (Proverbs 15:3). And the writer to the Hebrews explains, "Nothing in all creation is hidden from God. Everything is naked and exposed before his eyes, and he is the one to whom we are accountable" (Hebrews 4:13).

You never know if another human being is watching. Not long ago Becca and I went to a New Year's Eve celebration in Sydney, Australia, with about a million people. At one point I remarked, "There's not a soul here who knows us." Within seconds, I heard a voice behind us, "Pastor Rob, is that you?" Becca and I weren't doing anything we needed to hide, but it was still a surprise that some people in our church were only a few feet away . . . on the other side of the world. I couldn't believe it then, and I still can't believe it: What were the odds of people who recognized us sitting only a few feet away in that enormous crowd in Sydney? It still blows my mind!

No Harm No Foul

When I was overweight, I didn't have a flashing sign on my forehead showing my current level of cholesterol, and I avoided the scales to check my actual weight. As long as I remained ignorant of the hard realities, I felt confident. I had no idea that I was a ticking time bomb!

A lot of people in debt don't look at their bank balance or their credit card statements, and people in conflict just avoid any interactions with the other person. Or more commonly, people in strained or abusive relationships insist "everything is just fine" because shining a light on the problem will only make matters worse, at least in the short term. A common statement counselors make is, "What you resist persists." *Forbes* senior contributor Kathy Caprino lists several reasons people refuse to face hard realities, including: They minimize—"It's not that bad." They deflect—"It's not fair. Why do I have to be the one who has to change?" They excuse—"He couldn't help it. That's just the way he is." And they use magical thinking—"It'll get better. I just know it."[10] These are tried and true excuses to keep from addressing real problems.

I'm Not as Bad as . . .

Comparison is a deadly game . . . even if we win! It's easy to justify our behavior by looking around at people who are worse so we can proudly say, "Well, at least I'm not like him (or her)!" We compare ourselves to the jerk in the next office or the caustic neighbor, and we feel pretty good about ourselves. But that jerk and that neighbor compare themselves to someone worse so they can be self-satisfied, and that person indulges in the next layer of comparison and pride, until ultimately, someone says, "At least

I'm not like Hitler!" Jesus told a parable that perfectly illustrates
this kind of self-delusion:

> Then Jesus told this story to some who had great confi-
> dence in their own righteousness and scorned everyone
> else: "Two men went to the Temple to pray. One was a
> Pharisee, and the other was a despised tax collector. The
> Pharisee stood by himself and prayed this prayer: 'I thank
> you, God, that I am not like other people—cheaters, sin-
> ners, adulterers. I'm certainly not like that tax collector! I
> fast twice a week, and I give you a tenth of my income.'"

Tax collectors were Jews who collaborated with the Romans
to get taxes (and some extra for themselves). They were consid-
ered traitors. So, in this story, the Pharisee compared himself to
a guy who was like Benedict Arnold, and he came out looking
good! But Jesus wasn't finished with the story:

> "But the tax collector stood at a distance and dared not
> even lift his eyes to heaven as he prayed. Instead, he beat
> his chest in sorrow, saying, 'O God, be merciful to me,
> for I am a sinner.' I tell you, this sinner, not the Pharisee,
> returned home justified before God. For those who ex-
> alt themselves will be humbled, and those who humble
> themselves will be exalted." (Luke 18:9-14)

When I read this story, I wonder if the two guys overheard
each other. If they did, I can imagine that the Pharisee's self-satis-
faction was heightened by the tax collector's humble confession,
and the tax collector probably didn't have warm and fuzzy feelings

about the self-righteous Pharisee! The Pharisee's comparison would drive them even further apart . . . and that's what happens in our relationships when we compare ourselves either positively, resulting in pride, or negatively, resulting in shame.

I would say, "Don't do it!" but the fact is that we all do it. Comparison has been a part of human dysfunction since the beginning of the human race. (In the first chapters of the Bible, we read the tragic story of two brothers, Cain and Abel. Cain was jealous and murdered his brother. Not exactly a great beginning for family relationships!) Now, with the Internet and social media, we compare ourselves with people all over the world! Here's my go-to perspective: I'm not trying to be better than you. I'm trying to look more like Jesus and be the best me I can be.

I'm not trying to be better than you. I'm trying to look more like Jesus and be the best me I can be.

I Wasn't Prepared

Years ago, I traveled to several parts of the world to train leaders as part of John Maxwell's Million Leaders Mandate, and in those days, I traveled alone. On one of those trips, I flew into St. Petersburg, Russia, and caught a cab to my hotel. As I checked in, a man in the lobby came over to me and asked, "Sir, can I get you anything to make your stay more comfortable—alcohol, pills, a woman? I can get you anything. Just let me know."

I reacted, "What! I'm a pastor! I don't want any of that."

He smiled and said, "Trust me. I get these things for everyone, including pastors."

I felt morally and emotionally attacked, so I went to my room to enjoy some peace and quiet. I put my suitcase down and turned on the television. There, blaring in full view, was a porn video! I quickly turned it off. I decided to get out of the hotel and go for a walk. I headed out the front door and turned onto Nevsky Prospect, one of the main roads in the city. All along the street there were pictures of naked women. It was like a porn truck blew up and scattered this stuff everywhere!

I went back to my room and immediately made two phone calls: to Becca and my accountability partner at our church. Telling them about the situation brought light into the darkness. I told them to ask me hard questions when I got back home. On that trip, I made a commitment to never travel alone again. I hadn't been prepared for this trip, but I wasn't going to make that mistake again. I've watched friends and heroes of mine lose so much when they fell into a temptation because they traveled alone and weren't prepared. My heart breaks for them, and I hope and pray for their restoration. Having someone go with me would cost more money, but not having that person could cost me everything.

The Christians in Corinth proved that they weren't prepared to live godly lives in their pagan city, so Paul had to reprimand them to put them on the right path. He didn't promise that God would shield them from temptation, but he promised that God would prepare them to face it: "The temptations in your life are no different from what others experience. And God is faithful. He will not allow the temptation to be more than you can stand. When you are tempted, he will show you a way out so that you can endure" (1 Corinthians 10:13). That's God's promise to us, too. The "way out" is to be prepared so we can respond in faith, strength, and wisdom.

This list of excuses reminds me of the kids' game, *Chutes and Ladders*. The goal is to make it all the way to the end, Square #100. Players spin the arrow to see how many squares they advance. If they stop at the bottom of a ladder, they climb the ladder and skip a bunch of squares, but if they stop at the top of a chute, they slide back down to a lower point. Wisdom is like the ladders; it helps us move farther and faster toward the goal of experiencing God's presence and power. Self-deception, and the excuses we use when we're deceived, are chutes that either knock us backwards or keep us from moving up. But of course, life isn't a game. It's serious, and our willingness to be transparent and honest about the chutes we encounter is essential.

THE MYTH OF OMNI

Most of us aren't even aware of the impact of progress in technology and medicine in our slide away from meaningful, lasting change. Knowledge, the speed of life, modern forms of communication, affluence, travel, and medical advances are marvels of our age. It was only forty years ago, the blink of the historical eye, that the Internet was born, and today there are over 1.7 billion websites. Our grandparents drove cars that resembled tanks, and they were glad to have them, but cars today have far more computing power than Apollo lunar landing modules. In the early part of the 19th century, people thought that they'd disintegrate if they moved faster than the speed of a horse. Today, we think nothing of speeding along at 70 miles an hour (or more) on the highway and 500 miles an hour in planes. Flying above us in the International Space Station, those guys are traveling at five miles every second! Probably no field has shown more progress than medicine. Quite by accident, Alexander Fleming discovered the antibiotic properties of penicillin in 1928, and today's doctors are using a staggering array of innovative therapies to treat virtually every disease and disability.

My point is that all these advances create a myth that we're bulletproof—we're faster, more informed, and stronger than ever, so we don't really need God all that much. When we trust in the amazing advances instead of trusting in God, we're surprised by life's struggles, and we're shocked when modern technology can't fix everything immediately.

We've already looked at the problems created by comparison, but let me add one more observation: Social media is the ultimate comparison speed trap, hooking us in with beautiful pictures or snarky political statements, and leaving us preoccupied with where we are on the pecking order of every person on the planet. A number of studies have found powerful links between social media preoccupation and the risk for loneliness, self-harm, depression, anxiety, and thoughts of suicide.[11]

Our culture's promise that we can be omnipresent, omniscient, and omnipotent is certainly attractive, but it's totally misleading. It can't fill the hole in our souls and give us the meaning we long for. Advances in our culture are amazing, but they pale in comparison to God's infinite goodness and greatness.

LEARNED HELPLESSNESS

At the beginning of the slide, people often believe they're gaining control by lying, hiding, blame-shifting, and the other methods I've described. Sooner or later, however, their confidence erodes and they feel powerless. This isn't the good kind of powerlessness that is part of humility, which leads to repentance, strength, and joy. This is the kind that grinds the person's soul, leaving only shame, helplessness, and hopelessness. Over time, these people have developed "learned helplessness," which becomes the ultimate excuse as they claim, "Nothing ever works for me. I can't do anything right. Nothing will ever change." And with that conclusion, nothing does.

This heart-crushing perspective can come from very different causes. Some people have suffered severe trauma, and passivity is their way to cope with the chaos and pain. But others have grown up in families where their parents have smothered them with directions and protection, resulting in the child believing he's not competent to handle life's difficulties.

The Good News of the gospel is that Christ not only forgives, He also gives us a new, strong identity. We're not helpless; we're God's beloved sons and daughters, we have the power of the Holy Spirit living inside us, and God has made all things new.

We're not helpless; we're God's beloved sons and daughters, we have the power of the Holy Spirit living inside us, and God has made all things new.

No matter how far we've slid, and no matter how long we've been sliding, God is offering new hope, a new path, and a new purpose. Those of us who have been close to giving up can take heart in David's turnaround:

> I waited patiently for the Lord to help me,
>> and he turned to me and heard my cry.
> He lifted me out of the pit of despair,
>> out of the mud and the mire.
> He set my feet on solid ground
>> and steadied me as I walked along.
> He has given me a new song to sing,
>> a hymn of praise to our God.
> Many will see what he has done and be amazed.
>> They will put their trust in the Lord. (Psalm 40:1-3)

The excuses I've described in this chapter are very, very common, and they're at least some of the main reasons people don't keep the change they've committed to. Of course, we don't use them equally. We may use one or two more than the others, but somewhere in this chapter, I'm confident you've seen your picture.

Ninety-nine percent of the failures come from people who have the habit of making excuses.

—George Washington Carver

CONSIDER THIS:

1. Put this quote in your own words: "Self-deception is like this. It blinds us to the true causes of problems, and once we're

blind, all the 'solutions' we can think of will actually make matters worse. Whether at work or at home, self-deception obscures the truth about ourselves, corrupts our view of others and our circumstances, and inhibits our ability to make wise and helpful decisions."

2. What might be some reasons King Saul failed to recognize his slide, even though he had plenty of warnings?

3. Which of the excuses do you think are the most powerful? Explain your answer.

4. Which ones have your family members used? What are the consequences?

5. What's the sick but powerful connection between "blame throwers" and "blame sponges"? Describe their love-hate relationship.

6. Where did you see your picture in this chapter? Explain your answer.

7. Being vulnerable carries a significant measure of risk. Who can you be honest with about the excuses you've identified? What difference will it make to share your story and your heart with that person?

CHAPTER 3

◢ VIRTUE SIGNALING

The beauty of the impostor syndrome is you
vacillate between extreme egomania and a
complete feeling of: "I'm a fraud! Oh God,
they're on to me! I'm a fraud!" . . . just try to
ride the egomania when it comes and enjoy it,
and then slide through the idea of fraud.

—Tina Fey

*P*osturing. To some degree, all of us do it. After all, who is secure and confident enough to let people know who we really
are in the depths of our souls . . . when we don't even know what's
there? The imposter syndrome and virtue signaling are flip sides
of the same coin: The imposter syndrome is the sense that what
we've presented to the world is a sham—under the façade, we're
plagued with self-doubt, insecurity, and the fear of being found
out. And virtue signaling is the public expression of opinions to
impress, earn support, or display moral superiority—it's the way
we cover up and compensate for our insecurities.

On a larger scale, some companies and business leaders have
been caught in bold and sophisticated lies to fool investors and
consumers. A short list would include Enron, WorldCom, Bernie
Madoff, Tom Petters, Wells Fargo, and Volkswagen. In a *Harvard
Business Review* article, Ron Carucci quotes a disgruntled em-
ployee of a prominent company, "Our priorities change by the

week. Nobody wants to admit we're in trouble, so we're grasping at straws. We don't know who we are anymore, so we're just making things up." Carucci comments,

> Organizations in situations like this often double down on outdated strategies or reflexively reach for unrealistic strategic aspirations. They tout values and missions to rally confused employees. . . . When there is no effective process to gather decision makers into honest conversations about tough issues, truth is forced underground, leaving the organization to rely on rumors and gossip. Meetings are often seen as a waste of time because it's often unclear why they're taking place or who gets to make decisions. In one study, 71% of senior managers viewed meetings as unproductive and inefficient. We found that when effective governance is missing, organizations are 3.03 times more likely to have people withhold or distort information.[12]

On a far smaller level, individuals try to compensate for insecurities by projecting confidence and certainty. These messages often come across with an air of superiority: "I'm smart and you're dumb," "I'm right and you're wrong," "I'm on top and you're never going to replace me." This stance isn't about truth; it's about power. Winning is the goal, not understanding, kindness, and building up others even if they disagree.

What does this have to do with keeping the change? Quite a lot! When we invest our time and energy in posturing to cover our insecurities, we're not open to correction. In fact, we're not even open to a second opinion. We know we're right (We *have to be* right!), and we're not going to budge an inch.

When we invest our time and energy in posturing to cover our insecurities, we're not open to correction. In fact, we're not even open to a second opinion.

Does this happen in the spiritual and religious realms? You bet! The Pharisees were masters at virtue signaling. They were the original "holier than thou" folks. At many points, they criticized Jesus and His disciples for not following their additional rules about all kinds of rituals. It seems they always had another rule for people to follow . . . so they could put the fear of God in them if they didn't do everything exactly right. But actually, it wasn't the fear of God—it was the fear of being ridiculed and excluded by these religious bullies. Finally, it seems, Jesus had had enough. Matthew's Gospel records a string of Jesus' corrections directed at the rigid, heartless Pharisees. He told the people,

> "They crush people with unbearable religious demands and never lift a finger to ease the burden.
>
> "Everything they do is for show. On their arms they wear extra wide prayer boxes with Scripture verses inside, and they wear robes with extra long tassels. And they love to sit at the head table at banquets and in the seats of honor in the synagogues. . . .

"What sorrow awaits you teachers of religious law and you Pharisees. Hypocrites! For you are careful to tithe even the tiniest income from your herb gardens, but you ignore the more important aspects of the law—justice, mercy, and faith. You should tithe, yes, but do not neglect the more important things. Blind guides! You strain your water so you won't accidentally swallow a gnat, but you swallow a camel! . . .

"What sorrow awaits you teachers of religious law and you Pharisees. Hypocrites! For you are like whitewashed tombs—beautiful on the outside but filled on the inside with dead people's bones and all sorts of impurity. Outwardly you look like righteous people, but inwardly your hearts are filled with hypocrisy and lawlessness." (Matthew 23:4-6, 23-24, 27-28)

Jesus didn't pull any punches. He went right to their hearts and exposed their motives as well as their actions. It's entirely possible to do the right things for totally wrong reasons. Jesus pointed out that many of their actions weren't wrong, but their motives were far from the heart of God. Earlier in Matthew's account, Jesus addressed the problem of virtue signaling when He pointed out that people may give, pray, and fast "to be admired by others" instead of doing these things to please the Father (Matthew 6:1). And later in the sermon, He was even more pointed: "Not everyone who calls out to me, 'Lord! Lord!' will enter the Kingdom of Heaven. Only those who actually do the will of my Father in heaven will enter. On judgment day many will say to me, 'Lord! Lord! We prophesied in your name and cast out demons in your name and performed many miracles in your name.' But I will reply, 'I

never knew you. Get away from me, you who break God's laws'"
(Matthew 7:21-23).

These are chilling passages, especially for those who have
been actively serving in churches for a number of years. Jesus is
saying that it's possible to go through all the motions but miss
God's heart. These passages (and many others) may be painful
at first, but they're gracious invitations to open our hearts to experience far more of God's love and grace than ever before. It's
this deep heart transformation that enables us to keep the change.
(So, if you're disgusted with people who are into virtue signaling,
you're in good company. God doesn't like it either! Jesus talked
about it long before it became a thing on social media.)

It's this deep heart transformation that enables us to keep the change.

VULNERABILITY: THE THREAT AND THE HOPE

It's a paradox. We're terrified of anyone, including God,
knowing what's really going on in the depths of our hearts, but
the only way to heal the hurts and turn weakness into strength is
to expose our pain and weakness to the light. Vulnerability, then,
is usually seen as a curse, but it's an essential part of the cure.

Over the years when I've met with couples for marriage
counseling, it has been almost a universal experience that one
of them admitted he or she had a huge problem that needed to
be addressed, but the other would shrug and say, "It's not that
bad. We're fine." I've found that if I change the label of my role to

"marriage coach," the resistant one is much more willing to participate. The term "coach" doesn't imply weakness and deficiency, but it communicates that progress is needed. I've also noticed that sometimes the person who gets good marriage coaching tells friends, "My *counselor* is awesome!" Whatever works . . .

Hiding our needs is a way to prevent the threat of feeling vulnerable, but it shuts off avenues of care. For instance, our staff team received a note from someone in our church who wrote, "Please pray for me. I haven't recovered from my surgery yet." When I asked a question or two, I found out that the surgery was a month before, and they never told anyone. On the other hand, I live tweeted my heart attack from the back of an ambulance! I didn't try to hide my problem, and I didn't hide my desire for help.

Sometimes, our vulnerability overwhelms us. On October 24, 2013, my wife Becca's sister Naomi passed away of liver failure. Becca gave the eulogy at the funeral; it was a very sad day. A few weeks later, Becca and I were in Phoenix at a leadership retreat for our church staff, and we drove past the bank where Naomi had worked. At that moment, Becca just lost it, and the flood of sorrow was more than she could handle. Her pain didn't go away quickly at all. A week later at our Christmas party, one of our young interns asked Becca the simple question, "How are you doing?" and Becca melted down. Thankfully, my mom was at the party, and she asked Becca to go outside and take a walk to comfort her. On the walk, Becca must have said some things that really worried my mom because she made Becca promise she wouldn't do anything to harm herself.

It was evident that Becca needed to see a therapist. I asked, "Do you want to see somebody a long way from here where no one knows us?" (I wasn't sure how far we'd have to go. After all, people who knew us were in Sydney on New Year's Eve! It's really hard to go farther than that.)

She was at a point where protecting her image was no longer a priority. She responded, "I just want to get better."

We made an appointment, and I went with Becca. Sure enough, as soon as we opened the door to the waiting room, we saw a couple who attended our church. Instantly, both of them said, "Hey, Rob! Hey, Becca! So good to see you."

Becca didn't try to hide anything. She immediately announced, "I'm not doing well. I'm here for counseling." Which was, by the way, abundantly obvious. Why else would we be in a counselor's waiting room? I had wondered if Becca would be embarrassed to be seen there, but there wasn't even a hint of that. She was ready to do business with God, the counselor, and anyone else who could help her.

I know no one would believe this, but I talked the whole time during the hour with the therapist, so near the end of our time, she looked at me and said, "Rob, this is not your counseling session. You can't come back. I'll help Becca wade through all of this."

In the next session, the counselor assured Becca that she wasn't going crazy. The news was an incredible relief to her because she had wondered if her deep depression, racing thoughts, and feelings of hopelessness were irreversible. The counselor gave Becca two things that were incredibly valuable: assurance and tools. She explained how the body reacts to stress and trauma, she told Becca that her symptoms were a normal reaction to great loss, and she gave her some breathing techniques to use when she felt a panic attack coming on.

The backstory is that Naomi was an alcoholic. Becca had invited her to church for several years, but she always found excuses to avoid coming. Finally, when she showed up at our door, we were alarmed because her skin had a yellow tinge. She explained that she had just stopped drinking the week before, and she was having trouble with her liver during her detox. She came to church a few days later, and she sat near my mom. Naomi was struggling to concentrate, and my mom thought she was drunk. The Lord gave my mom insight, though, that Naomi was sick, not drunk. Mom invited her to step into the lobby to talk, and there, my mom prayed with Naomi and she said "Yes" to Jesus. Three days later, she was admitted to the hospital with liver failure, and she never left. She died a month later. We were in Phoenix only weeks after that.

As you can tell so far in my own stories, I'm pretty much an open book, but I wanted to protect Becca from being exposed in her deep grief and loss. She didn't care in the least. She was willing to be completely vulnerable with me, with the couple in the waiting room, with the counselor, and with anyone else who wanted to know what was going on with her. When she shared this story in our church, God used her vulnerability to bring God's healing and hope to people who had lived with intense pain, compounded by shame for being "weak" and "flawed" for suffering with the pain for many years.

BROKEN POTS

The paradox of the Christian life is that to be forgiven, we have to admit that we're sinners; to experience the wonder of God's love, we have to admit that we were His enemies; to be healed and whole, we have to admit we're broken. The gospel is bad news before it's good news. If we aren't deeply aware of our self-sufficiency, our apathy, or our rebellion toward God, we won't embrace His love, forgiveness, power, and purpose.

In Paul's second letter to the Corinthians (actually, it's almost certainly his third letter, but the second one is believed to be lost), he points them to the wonder of the gospel: "For God, who said, 'Let light shine out of darkness,' made his light shine in our hearts to give us the light of the knowledge of God's glory displayed in the face of Christ" (2 Corinthians 4:6 NIV). He then changes the metaphor from light to pottery to explain the paradox: "But we have this treasure in jars of clay to show that this all-surpassing power is from God and not from us" (v. 7). The gospel of grace is God's greatest treasure, worth more than all the gold, oil, real estate, and other valuables the world has ever or will ever know, but the carrying case for this treasure is something very humble—in fact, clay pots, you and me. This insight enables us to be both vulnerable and courageous. Sometimes we can be vulnerable but not courageous—weak and helpless. And sometimes we can be courageous but not vulnerable—tough and demanding. But grace invites us to be completely honest about our flaws, our weaknesses, and our sins because it assures us of God's forgiveness, kindness, and purpose.

Those who hold vulnerability in one hand and the treasure in the other have the amazing capacity to handle anything life throws at them. Paul put it this way: "We are hard pressed on every side, but not crushed; perplexed, but not in despair; persecuted, but not abandoned; struck down, but not destroyed. We always carry around in our body the death of Jesus, so that the life of Jesus may also be revealed in our body" (vv. 8-10).

Do you want to be strong? Be vulnerable enough to admit your weakness. Do you want to experience God's love more than ever before? Be vulnerable to admit you don't deserve it. Do you want a life of measureless meaning? Be vulnerable to admit your life is empty without God.

Do you want to be strong? Be vulnerable enough to admit your weakness.

Most of us are sure that if people really knew us, they wouldn't love us . . . and they wouldn't like us, respect us, or want to hang out with us. That's the imposter syndrome. We're sure they'd run away, make fun of us, or throw rocks at us. But the gospel says that God knows the very worst about us—the things we hope no one ever finds out—and He loves us still. Corrie ten Boom saw the best and the worst in people at Ravensbrück concentration camp in Nazi Germany. She watched as her sister Betsie died in the camp. If a group of people ever felt exposed and vulnerable, it was the prisoners there, yet when it was over, Corrie had a testimony of faith and hope: "There is no pit so deep, that God's love is not deeper still."[13] That truth applies whether others have thrown us in a pit or when the pit is of our own making.

Our natural inclination is to hide our flaws and weaknesses. The Bible tells us that when Adam and Eve sinned, they covered themselves and tried to hide from God, and we've followed their example ever since. The fear of exposure leads to lying and manipulating others to give us what we want from them, and when they resent this pressure, we feel isolated. The courage to be vulnerable—with trustworthy, wise, loving people—has the opposite effect: we can be brutally honest about ourselves, we learn to love with no strings attached, and we develop strong relationships. But make no mistake, not everyone is safe.

If you've been hurt by an authority figure, especially parents, it's understandable to hesitate to be vulnerable with the ultimate authority figure: God. One of my roles as a pastor is to assure those who have been deeply hurt in relationships that God is far more loving, far more compassionate, and far more patient and kind than they can imagine. Jesus' emotion most described in the gospels is His compassion. Often it says "he was moved with compassion." This means it wasn't a surface feeling. His love, kindness, and care as He looked at people in need shook Him to His core. That's how He looks at you when you're in pain.

The prophet Isaiah used two metaphors to illustrate God's compassion. In a passage about the Messiah who would come, he wrote, "A bruised reed he will not break, and a smoldering wick he will not snuff out. In faithfulness he will bring forth justice" (Isaiah 42:3 NIV). Jesus was exquisitely tender with those who were suffering. He's the same with us when we're in pain.

RED OR BLUE?

Over two decades ago, a movie came out about a young computer programmer named Thomas Anderson, known by his online alias Neo. In his job as a hacker, he runs across a word several times that has no meaning to him: *matrix*. He is contacted by a mysterious stranger and offered a choice: take a red pill and understand the truth about the Matrix, which is what's going on behind what normal people can see, or he can take a blue pill and forget everything he had learned about the truth under the surface. God is giving us a similar choice today. We can take the red pill of vulnerability and enter the amazing, glorious, and sometimes terrifying world of God's great love and His higher purpose for us, or we can take the blue pill and keep our heads in the sand, valuing the safety of denial more than the thrill of being fully known and deeply loved.

Which will you take? If you take the red pill and open your heart to God's truth about you, about himself, and about His kingdom, you'll be amazed at what you find. Everything is upside down: The Creator of billions of galaxies became a baby. The King of all became a servant. The Author of life swapped Hhis life for ours. The Healer was tortured. The Light died in the dark. Who did He do all this for? Sinners. Sinners like you and me. I love Paul's prayer in his letter to the Colossians. Half of it is about the wonder of grace: ". . . giving joyful thanks to the Father, who has qualified you to share in the inheritance of his holy people in the kingdom of light. For he has rescued us from the dominion of darkness and brought us into the kingdom of the Son he loves, in whom we have redemption, the forgiveness of sins" (Colossians 1:12-14 NIV).

We weren't pretty good people who need a little help to be right with God; we were *disqualified*, helpless and hopeless because of our sin. But the Father has qualified us through the sacrifice of His Son to be completely His, and He adopted us into His family to share in the inheritance of the riches of His grace. We were citizens of the domain of darkness, but God sent a rescue mission to bring us out and take us into Jesus' kingdom. We who were condemned because of our sin have been completely forgiven, and amazingly, Jesus' own righteousness has been credited to our account. That's what it means to be "in Christ." We're in Him in His perfect life, in Him in His death, in Him in His resurrection, and in Him in His ascension to the throne. When the Father looks at us, He looks through the lens of Jesus, and He delights in us.

When we're tempted to give up because keeping the change is too hard, we need to think about Jesus enduring for us. The writer to the Hebrews explains it like this:

> Therefore, since we are surrounded by such a huge crowd of witnesses to the life of faith, let us strip off every weight that slows us down, especially the sin that so easily trips us up. And let us run with endurance the race God has set before us. We do this by keeping our eyes on Jesus, the champion who initiates and perfects our faith. Because of the joy awaiting him, he endured the cross, disregarding its shame. Now he is seated in the place of honor beside God's throne. Think of all the hostility he endured from sinful people; then you won't become weary and give up. After all, you have not yet given your lives in your struggle against sin. (Hebrews 12:1-4)

What was "the joy awaiting him" on the other side of suffering and death on the cross? You . . . and me. The sacrifice was excruciatingly painful—physically and spiritually—but Jesus endured because He anticipated the sheer joy of welcoming you and me into the Father's family. When we look at how He endured in our place and for our sakes, we "won't become weary and give up" when we're trying to keep the change.

Grace is the invitation to be open and honest with God. It comes stamped with His assurance that His love is higher, His kindness is deeper, and His power is stronger than we can ever imagine. There is no fear in that love. Are you afraid of being vulnerable with God? Of course you are! But are you willing to take the plunge to trust Him with all of your dreams and dreads? I hope so. Actor Will Smith (that renowned theologian!) reminds us, "Everything you want is on the other side of fear." (I'm writing this only a couple of weeks after "the slap" at the Oscars. I would remind him of this quote so he can find peace again.)

I've faced weakness, uncertainty, and doubt many times in my life. Sometimes I've wavered, but most of the time, sooner or later, I took a step of faith. I'll tell you that the payoffs of taking these risks are enormous.

I've noticed that the right kind of *vulnerability* produces *stability* which results in *vitality*. How? When we're honest about our deficiencies, we open our hearts to God's grace. We realize we can't earn God's love, we can't do enough to impress Him, and we can't twist His arm. Grace is a gift or it's not grace. When we get off the treadmill of trying to prove we're worthy of God's love, we leave our pride and shame aside, and we find security, peace, and gratitude. And we also experience a fresh surge of energy. We're incredibly thankful to God, we want please Him, we want to honor Him, and we want His kingdom to flourish. But none of this happens without steps of vulnerability and the experience of God's grace.

God's grace opens a wide door to our experience of His presence and power. We realize He has given us supernatural abilities to touch lives and expand His kingdom, and as we walk with Him, the heart and character of Jesus is gradually produced in us. A sterile theology doesn't produce a changed life, it doesn't motivate us to serve selflessly, and it doesn't have a positive impact on the people around us. But having our hearts melted and molded by the love of God has multiplied effects that change us from the inside out, and in our joy and gratitude, God gives us the privilege of being His partners in the greatest enterprise the world has ever known: healing the brokenhearted, forgiving those who struggle with guilt, leading people who have lost their way, and giving hope to the hopeless—and inviting them all to join us in changing the world.

Becca wanted me to tell her story in this chapter because she has experienced the joy of being open, honest, and vulnerable. My guess is that you also have a story of heartache, perhaps one that has caused you to close your heart to God and people. Don't waste the pain. Let it prompt you to say, "God, I'm afraid, but I trust You to be tender with my heart. I want to experience more of Your grace. Touch me. Heal me. Fill me."

CONSIDER THIS:

1. How would you define and describe "the imposter syndrome"? Why do you think it's so powerful?

2. What are some ways virtue signaling enflames comparison and competition, and then harms relationships?

3. Why do you think people are afraid of being vulnerable? What are, in their minds, the risks?

4. Look again at 2 Corinthians 4:5-10. What difference does it make (or would it make) to see yourself as a clay pot holding the treasure of the gospel?

5. Which pill do you want to take? What's the risk in taking each one?

6. Explain how vulnerability produces stability which results in vitality.

CHAPTER 4

◢ AN UPWARD CURVE

There comes a moment when you must quit talking to God about the mountain in your life and start talking to the mountain about your God. You proclaim His power. You declare His sovereignty. You affirm His faithfulness. You stand on His Word. You cling to His promises.

—Mark Batterson

To keep the change, we need a powerful blend of two traits: *patience and tenacity*. Both. Not one or the other. If we're patient without being tenacious, we give ourselves too much room for error, and we employ the excuses far too often. But if we're tenacious without enough patience, we get so discouraged when we hit rough patches (which inevitably happen) that we want to quit. Very few of us have the perfect balance. It's important to know which way we lean . . . so we're not surprised when we lean too far, and so we can make changes more quickly and avoid major crashes.

The blend of patience and tenacity has a different look and feel depending on the change we're keeping. A lot of changes are *chronic*: weight, blood pressure, saving, spending, giving, time management, prioritizing family, and many others. As the saying goes, "You don't get fat in a day, and you don't get slim in a day."

We need to keep moving forward, realizing that the benefits will be seen over a long stretch of time.

But other changes are critical. If you've had an affair, your spouse won't be too impressed if you say, "I'm doing a little better this week!" Some habits require committed, dogged abstinence. If you're an alcoholic or an addict, one slip can send you reeling . . . and cause even more damage to the trust you're trying to rebuild with your family, supervisor, and friends. If you've embezzled money from your employer, taking a little less this month isn't a workable solution. If you're drowning in debt, spending a little less only adds to the problem. If people have abused you, it's not enough to ask them politely to do it less often and with a little less cruelty.

But other changes are critical. If you've had an affair, your spouse won't be too impressed if you say, "I'm doing a little better this week!"

Even in such critical changes, people slip up. I get that, but a relapse isn't permission to keep going into a freefall. It's a call to come back and start over again. Before he died not long ago, pastor Sy Rogers counseled a lot of men with sexual disorders. When he spoke at our church, he told us about a man who had been addicted to pornography. The man stopped for a week, but then he returned to his habit. He was devastated that he hadn't kept his commitment, but when he told Sy about it, Sy responded,

"A week! That's fantastic! Now, start over again." Sy's encouragement changed the man's perspective from hopeless to hopeful.

YOU SHALL NOT PASS!

My mom suffered verbal and emotional abuse in her relationship with her father. Her dad was in the military, and the only way he knew to relate to her was like a commanding officer. He was demanding, strict, and at the very low end of communicating love and affirmation. When she was a girl, he regularly went into her room for a thorough inspection. He put on white gloves and carefully examined everything—the top of the doorframe, the bookcase, the windowsill, and every other surface in the room. If her room wasn't spotless with everything perfectly stored and arranged, she received his stern reprimand and severe punishment. When she was old enough to go out with her friends, if she was one minute past the time her dad told her to be home, he grounded her. There was no grace. She has vaguely alluded to other things her dad did that were much more brutal and destructive, but she hasn't told me much about those. Mom's two brothers ran away from home. Their father had been physically abusive to them, as well as verbally and emotionally. It's not surprising that they wanted to get away as soon as possible and as far as possible. One of them was incarcerated as a teenager but later turned his life around, and the other was found dead, probably by suicide, on an island in Hawaii.

When I was a boy, my mother's parents sometimes came for visits. Before they arrived, Mom pleaded with me, "If you see that I'm alone with my dad, come sit in my lap. Don't let me be alone with him. Do you understand?" I understood what she was saying, but I had no idea why she was afraid of being alone with her own father.

My grandfather trusted in Christ and asked for forgiveness not long before he died. The family asked me to do the funeral, and I was glad to have the opportunity to tell people he had become a believer. For my mother, though, the event carried a very different meaning: she was finally free from the fear of being abused by her dad. His death brought profound relief, not grief. A few days after the service, she told me, "He can never hurt me again. I'm glad he found grace, but he was really mean to me. Now I'll no longer have to be afraid of him." She told me that at the funeral, a line from *The Wizard of Oz* played on repeat in her mind: "Ding-dong! The witch is dead!" If you think this sounds harsh and unfeeling, you probably don't know anyone who has suffered the kind of abuse my mother experienced. She was finally free from years of fear and heartache.

Let me put a few more pieces on the table to complete the puzzle. Before my mom met my dad, she was a flight attendant. She met an attractive pilot, and she got pregnant with his child. When the baby was born, she gave it up for adoption. For decades, she hid this truth from her dad because she was convinced he would never speak to her again if he found out. Mom had told her mother about the baby, but the two of them never breathed a word about it to her dad. The secret protected both of them from his wrath.

The baby girl was adopted and grew up. Many years later, her adoptive mother died, and she decided to look for her birth mom. She found my mother and introduced herself to our family. I was 18 years old. Mom tried to explain, "When I was a young woman, I got pregnant and had a daughter. I put her up for adoption, and now, after all these years, my daughter has found me. I never told your grandfather. I was just too scared."

My instant reaction was, "You're lying! That can't be true." Ironically, a short time before this conversation, I had looked at my birth certificate. (I probably needed it to apply for a sport I was interested in.) I insisted, "It says on my birth certificate, 'Number of previous births: ZERO.' That's how I know you're not telling the truth."

She calmly told me, "Rob, in the 60s, doctors would lie for you." She let that sink in for a few seconds and then came back to the main point: "You have a sister."

We welcomed Jeanine, my new sibling, into the family. As soon as I saw her, I did a double-take—she's the spitting image of my mom.

At that point, I understood why my mom was so dedicated to helping other people's children through foster care. She was doing for them what someone had done for her in her moment of heartache, confusion, and fear. For years, she lived with the reality that she had a daughter somewhere, but Mom didn't know how her child was navigating life. Finally, by God's grace and in His timing, Mom discovered what had happened to her.

I grew up with three brothers, but one year my dad gave my mom a birthstone ring with five stones. I remember asking him, "Dad, why did you get a ring with five stones? Did you forget how many children you have?"

He smiled and said, "Oh, the fifth one is for the foster girls your mom loves." I found out later that he had known the whole time, and he put the fifth stone in the ring to honor the relationship between Mom and the sister I'd never known.

To bring it full circle, the pain my mother suffered in her relationship with her daughter and the loss she experienced in giving her up for adoption were translated into a life of compassion for children who don't have a safe home. She could have withered emotionally and become a helpless victim, but she turned her sorrow into practical, loving care for kids who are some of the most vulnerable people in our society. Mom's pain gave her the tenacity to let God use her to change lives. She had to be both patient with the process of emotional healing and tenacious in pursuing God's love, grace, and kindness.

For me, one of the most memorable scenes in all the movies I've watched is in *Lord of the Rings: Fellowship of the Ring*. Gandalf, the old wise wizard, has been leading Frodo and the others on their journey to take the ring back to Mordor. At a critical point, the vicious and powerful Balrog demon pursues them. Gandalf raises his staff and crashes it down, yelling to the demon, "You cannot pass! I am a servant of the Secret Fire, wielder of the Flame of Anor. The dark fire will not avail you, Flame of Udun! Go back to the shadow. You shall not pass!" I can envision my mother looking at her four young sons, remembering the threat of my grandfather's abusive anger. At some point—or more likely, at many points—I can imagine her standing in front of that threat to those she loved, and in godly defiance yelling, "You shall not pass!"

Mom broke the mold. She changed the trajectory of our family history. She—and people like her—are some of the most courageous people on earth. The abuse she suffered could have ended terribly for her, and through the multiplication of her pain, for my brothers and me, but she didn't let that happen. I always knew my mom was special, but when I learned more of her story, I found that she's a true hero.

Mom broke the mold. She changed the trajectory of our family history. She—and people like her—are some of the most courageous people on earth.

REALISM AND HOPE

I know some people who have gone through dark, dark times and come out stronger and wiser on the other side. Sometimes the darkness was their own making, and sometimes they were victims of others' selfishness and cruelty. Whatever the source, these brave people set aside the many excuses and simplistic solutions. They became ruthlessly realistic, willing to look at themselves and the damage they've done or the hurt they've suffered, and they've found a deep source of persistent hope, trusting that a good God will bring light into the darkness.

The default mode of the human heart is self-justification. We want to prove that we're worthy of love, good enough to earn respect, decent enough to win approval. However, those who have come to the end of themselves are no longer under such illusions. They realize they're lost. When the amazing, unmerited grace of God is presented to them, some assume they're beyond God's love, and they turn away. Others think it's too good to be true. And still others are stunned that the God of the universe would know the worst about them and love them still. God's love takes root in these people, and they're transformed by the power of the Spirit from the inside out.

Like my mother, people who experience the wonder of grace see the world as upside down. All around us are people who pursue pleasure, power, and popularity at all costs, and our culture reinforces these idols. These things in themselves aren't wrong, but when we make secondary things our heart's primary pursuit, we've put them in God's rightful place. But when God's matchless love changes us, everything is different. We find this throughout the Scriptures:

> To have true purpose, let go of your plans and embrace God's design for your life: "If you try to hang on to your life, you will lose it. But if you give up your life for my sake, you will save it" (Matthew 16:25).

> If you want to be great, be a servant: "You know that the rulers in this world lord it over their people, and officials flaunt their authority over those under them. But among you it will be different. Whoever wants to be a leader among you must be your servant, and whoever wants to be first among you must become your slave" (Matthew 20:25-27).

> Those who insist on positions of prominence will be taken down a notch or two . . . or more: "So those who are last now will be first then, and those who are first will be last" (Matthew 20:16).

> The results of selfish ambition are counterproductive. "But those who exalt themselves will be humbled, and those who humble themselves will be exalted" (Matthew 23:12).

> True riches come from radical generosity: "You must each decide in your heart how much to give. And don't give reluctantly or in response to pressure. 'For God loves a person who gives cheerfully.' And God will generously provide all you need. Then you will always have everything you need and plenty left over to share with others" (2 Corinthians 9:7-8).

> To experience the depths and heights of God's love, forgiveness, and acceptance, realize that these are gifts of grace, not things you can earn by being good enough (1 John 4:10-11; Ephesians 4:31—5:2; Romans 15:7).

Does this perspective, this heart change, seem out of reach? It is, until we see that Jesus embodied all of these traits, and more. The Beatitudes in the opening verses of the Sermon on the Mount (Matthew 5:3-10) aren't just ethical requirements for Christians. If we see them in light of the rest of Matthew's account of the life of Jesus, we see something far deeper, far richer, and far more motivating than ethical standards:

> Jesus, the Creator of the universe, became *poor in spirit* to open the door of God's kingdom to us and make us spiritually rich beyond all measure.

> On the cross, Jesus *mourned* the loss of the Father's presence and cried out, "My God, my God, why have you forsaken me?" so we could experience the warmth and comfort of the Father.

> Jesus *humbled* himself, "emptied himself," and submitted to ridicule, torture, and death so we could inherit the highest honor of being God's beloved children.

> As He was dying, Jesus said, "I thirst." His thirst for *righteousness* and justice led Him to Calvary, where He bore God's judgment instead of meting out God's judgment on sinners like us.

> On the cross, Jesus even had *mercy* for those who were killing Him. He prayed, "Father, forgive them for they don't know what they're doing." When we experience His mercy, we pay it forward to those who need it.

> Jesus was *pure in heart*, but His perfection didn't make Him rigid and demanding. He was the most joyful person the world has ever known because He was always aware of the presence of the Father.

> Jesus' *peace* was shattered at Gethsemane and Calvary as He bore our sins and experienced the hell we deserve, so that we can enjoy the peace of God.

> Jesus suffered every form of *persecution*, not because He was harsh and demanding, but because the religious leaders felt threatened by His love and miraculous power. When we walk with Him, some people will applaud, some will marvel, and some will despise us. But our courage and kindness will show that our citizenship is in heaven.[14]

When our hearts are riveted on "the right-side-up kingdom" of pleasure, power, and popularity, we try hard to get what we want, and we're frustrated with God if He doesn't come through to give us what we're sure we deserve. To a great extent, we're creatures of our culture: we absorb the values of the people, organizations, and media around us—but it doesn't have to stay that way. We can be ruthlessly realistic about the impact of the culture, including the environment created in our families, and we can be tenaciously hopeful because Jesus gave himself, loving us "to the end." Getting even a glimpse of His sacrifice for us melts us, molds us, and motivates us to live for Him.

Some of us, though, have difficulty understanding and experiencing the love of God. It's a fundamental concept of developmental psychology that children are deeply affected by their relationship with their parents. Those who grow up in stable, loving, honest homes are still sinners in need of God's grace, but they have a leg up on many others. They don't need perfect parents, but they've benefited from what family experts call "good enough parents."[15] Tony Brown is one of the songwriters of "[You're a] Good Good Father." When some people hear the song, they think, *Yes, God is like my dad. He loves me and wants the best for me!* But people who have been abused or abandoned have a radically skewed view of God. They, too, assume He's like their parents. When they hear the lyrics of that song, they think, *Uh, not so fast. Convince me.* Instead of comparing the Father's love and care with their earthy father, they have to draw a contrast: *God isn't like my dad or my mom. He's not abusive, He's not distant. He's present, tender, and strong. He loves me, and I can trust Him.* And that's exactly what Tony Brown did. He grew up never knowing his dad. In an interview, he explains, "The only one I've ever called 'Father' is

God. Just saying [the word good] once was not enough," so it's repeated. "The song helps you unlearn damaging things you have heard about God."[16]

My mother's story, or something like it, may not be anything close to your experience, but I assure you that you know people who have suffered unimaginable wounds at the hands of those who were responsible to love and protect them. How can you know who has stories like that? Ask people to tell you about their childhood experiences. If they hesitate, lose eye contact, and insist that everything was "just fine," they may be living with dark secrets (or they may be late for an appointment and are simply blowing you off). Hopefully, you'll build enough trust for them to begin to open the door on their past, even slightly at first, so they can begin to experience healing, hope, and love.

EMS

How does the curve change? What has to happen for the trajectory of a person to start moving up? We'll look at some very practical steps later in the book, but here I want to focus on the kind of resources we need to heal any deep emotional and spiritual wounds. We begin with the fact that we have two conditions: we're sinners and we're wounded. The cross of Christ resolves the first problem. His grace is greater than all our sin. For those who have deep and festering wounds, the process of change is a bit different.

Think of it this way: Those of us who have been emotionally damaged through childhood hurts, betrayal, affairs, or divorce are like a person lying on the side of the road after a car wreck. He has compound breaks and internal injuries. Someone calls 9-1-1, and in minutes, an ambulance arrives at the scene. The paramedics stabilize the person's limbs, hook up monitors, and load him into the ambulance. When they arrive at the hospital, an ER doc examines him, cleans him up, and wheels him into surgery to set the broken bones. He stays in the hospital for a while to regain some strength, and then he begins the rehab process. Based on the testimony of many people, rehabilitation is the hardest part of healing. Day after day, the occupational therapist takes the person through exercises to strengthen atrophied muscles and increase flexibility. Every day, the injured person wants to quit, but he shows up and does another set of exercises. At first, he uses crutches, then a walker, then a cane, and finally, he walks . . . but with a limp. If anyone asks him about his limp, he says, "Oh man, this is real progress! You should have seen me right after the wreck. I wasn't sure I'd walk again. In fact, I wasn't sure I'd live!"

I've seen this pattern of brokenness, intervention, professional care, and the long, slow process of healing in the lives of countless people who have suffered PTSD, childhood horrors, strained marriages, prodigal children, addictions, and many other relational wounds. In some cases, the wound happened in a moment, but in others, the hurt, fear, anger, and shame accumulated to create constant, unwelcome companions. Whatever the source of the problem, God walks with us through the process of experiencing His love more deeply so we can grieve our losses, forgive those who have hurt us, and heal the broken places. Sometimes, God works a miracle and the healing is fast, but more often, the miracle is seen in God's kindness and faithfulness to those who mend slowly.

PHONE A FRIEND

God has made us relational people. We're meant to be together, and charting an upward trendline to keep the change requires support and encouragement. My dad was that person for my mom, but it doesn't always work that way! Quite often, both people in a marriage bring so much baggage that it takes years for them to work through the hurt created by misplaced expectations and fragile egos. But God gave my mom a great gift in my dad. Some people say men marry someone like their moms and women marry someone like their dads, but my father was the polar opposite of my mom's dad. It was devastating when my dad died of cancer when he was 65. Mom once confided, "I have friends who don't even like their husbands, and those men live into their 80s. I was madly in love with this amazing guy, and he died far too young."

There are particular breakthroughs you can't experience without having someone actively involved in your life. All of the "one another" passages in the Bible imply that God's truth can only be applied in open, supportive relationships. For instance, we can't be patient with one another unless we're close enough to be annoyed.

We're wounded in relationships, and we're healed in relationships. In other words, grace has a face.

We're wounded in relationships, and we're healed in relationships. In other words, grace has a face. That person—at least one, but probably no more than a few—represents Jesus to us. We learn that Jesus is full of compassion when that person doesn't laugh, run away, or blast us with ridicule when we're vulnerable about our fears and faults.

Some of us read the Bible and see only demands and condemnation. We need new lenses to see the heart of Jesus in the pages of Scripture. He touched the untouchables. In the first chapter of Mark's Gospel, a leper knelt at Jesus' feet and pleaded, "If you are willing, you can heal me and make me clean." In that day, people stayed away from lepers, and lepers were commanded to steer clear of people who didn't have the disease. I'm sure people were stunned when this guy with rotting flesh knelt in front of Jesus, but look what happened: "Moved with compassion, Jesus reached out and touched him. 'I am willing,' he said. 'Be healed!' Instantly the leprosy disappeared, and the man was healed" (Mark 1:40-42).

No religious leader would touch a leper because it would instantly make him ceremonially unclean. He wouldn't be allowed to go to the temple, he wouldn't be able to offer sacrifices, and he would be excluded from fellowship with God's people. But when Jesus took the initiative to touch the man, Jesus didn't become unclean. Instead, the man became clean! Jesus summons us: "Follow me." What does that mean? Many things, but it certainly means that we move toward the people who are "unclean" in our communities, the ones who may be rich in possessions but lepers in spirit, those who feel like outcasts in a crowd, those who have messed up so badly that those close to them no longer trust them, those who are lying on the side of life's highway broken and bruised.

I know, I know. A lot of people believe the church is full of judgmental hypocrites who are eager to put the hammer down on anyone who doesn't measure up to our high standards. There probably are churches like that, but I haven't been in any of them. Instead, I've seen people in churches who have the heart of Jesus for the down-and-out who have lost hope, as well as the up-and-coming whose pride will one day be shattered and they'll need a friend. No one is off-limits to God's love—not the leper in this story who was healed, and not Zacchaeus the rich tax collector who trusted in Jesus and became generous (Luke 19:1-10). Most churches are filled with people who are learning what it means to experience God's grace so deeply that we want to represent Him to everyone we meet.

 **Rob Ketterling**
@robketterling   ...

Christians aren't perfect, they're "perfecting". They're simply on a journey to allow grace to change them for the better.

9:12 AM · Oct 21, 2014 · Twitter for iPhone

The trendline of the curve may be very different for different people. Some find themselves at a negative 10, and they show amazing progress to get to 0. Others have greater resources of parental love and confidence, and their trendline goes from 2 to 7. We're not comparing where we are; we're just looking at how far we've come.

If we try to change on our own, we can certainly make some progress, but self-effort seldom leads to satisfactory outcomes. We need two essential ingredients: *grace and a friend*. With them, God can work miracles (even if they slowly unfold); without them, we have plenty of starts and stops, and we get frustrated that we aren't making more progress.

We live in the most connected age the world has ever known, but we paradoxically are suffering an epidemic of loneliness. We may think primarily of older people who live alone as those who feel the pangs of being alone, but a Pew Research Survey reported that Gen Z adults—those born between 1997 and 2012, and particularly those who are older in that range—are the loneliest. A Stanford University article states:

> In fact, those aged 18 to 22 have the highest loneliness scores.... Loneliness has significant health consequences for all age groups. Julianne Holt-Lunstad, a psychology professor at Brigham Young University, found that loneliness and social isolation can be as damaging to peoples' health as smoking 15 cigarettes a day and contributes to early mortality. Other studies show that those who identify themselves as lonely are 59 percent more likely to lose the ability to perform daily living tasks, and are at higher risk of cardiovascular disease, obesity, dementia, and depression.[17]

I'm sure some people have meaningful connections through social media, but far too many of us present a dry-cleaned version of ourselves and our interests. The gap between *supposed* friends and *real* friends leaves us knowing we're fakes, far less than authentic, which is the highest value in today's world. The time we spend online has, to some degree, eroded our ability to have face-to-face interactions that deepen connections. The posts we view make our lives seem dull and boring so that jealousy and envy become problematic. Spending too much time online distracts us from real relationships and raises the incidence of anxiety and depression. Comparing ourselves to the most beautiful and handsome people on the planet makes us feel ugly and inadequate. And carefully posed shots of a delicious dish tell us that we're losers for eating Ramen noodles. But none of these traits are listed in the fruit of the Spirit in Paul's letter to the Galatians!

When we look at the stories in the Scriptures, we see some endearing and enduring relationships that enabled people's lives to curve upward. For instance, where would David have been without Jonathan's sacrificial love for him when David became an outcast from Saul's court? And what would have happened to David if Nathan hadn't had the courage to step in to confront him about his sin? We usually think of Paul as a fierce follower of Jesus, but he almost always had someone with him on his journeys: Barnabas, Silas, Timothy, and Epaphroditus, to name a few.

I'm convinced that God is more than willing to meet us where we are, impart His great grace when we feel vulnerable, and bring at least one person to us to help us grow. In fact, as I read the Bible, it seems that God takes special delight in changing the trajectory of those who have fallen the furthest. If you're one of those, take heart. God is waiting for you!

We all want progress, but if you're on the wrong road, progress means doing an about-turn and walking back to the right road; in that case, the man who turns back soonest is the most progressive.

—C.S. Lewis

CONSIDER THIS:

1. How would you describe the necessity of having both patience and tenacity as we keep the change?

2. What kind of changes are *critical*—to correct behaviors that need to be avoided at all costs? And what are some changes that are *chronic* and require a long-term view of progress? In which category do your changes fall?

3. Emotional pain can cause a person to collapse, become defiant, or learn wisdom. Do you know people in each category? What are the lessons from the ones who learned wisdom from their heartache?

4. Look again at the passages that describe the "upside-down" life and the passages that explain how Jesus exemplified this life to the nth degree. What do these truths tell us about the source of inner conviction and strength?

5. How is emotional and spiritual healing like someone being picked up after a terrible car wreck? Do know anyone in that long process? What does that person need to keep moving forward?

6. What does it mean to you that Jesus touched the untouchables? Do you see yourself as the leper in the story, as one of the horrified religious leaders who steered clear of the man, or as a disciple learning to follow Jesus' example? Explain your answer.

7. Do you have a friend like the Bible describes in Jonathan, Nathan, or Timothy? If you do, what impact has that person had on you? If not, where can you find this kind of friend?

CHAPTER 5

◢ LAZARUS TIME

> Don't think there are no second chances. Life
> always offers you a second chance. . . . It's
> called "tomorrow."
>
> *— Nicholas Sparks*

In the middle of the early lockdowns during the Covid pandemic, our church tried to figure out how to connect with people without hosting super-spreader events. The pandemic was a strain for individuals, families, businesses, and churches—no one was exempt from the uncertainty and fear.

During this time, our facilities director, Scott Olson, died after a battle with cancer. When we held his funeral outside at the gravesite, his wife Leslie told us about her loving, courageous husband, and she shared more about their response to his diagnosis. She said, "We asked God for more time . . . an extension of our days together. As we moved through those early days, the Holy Spirit very clearly spoke to my heart and said, 'Leslie, do you know what Lazarus's miracle was? It was simply a miracle of more time. I gave Lazarus more time, Leslie, but he did eventually die.' Over the next months, I was able to see that we were living on the gift of Lazarus time. Scott and I had our eyes open to see those gifts from God." Leslie concluded, "I wanted to share these moments because I think we all face them daily—the choice to do or believe the right thing. We live in a culture that cripples us with decision fatigue, but we can't get carried away by those waves. We have to stay on our feet and listen for the voice of God. I want people to know what we learned: we need to choose Him each and every moment."

Scott wasn't defined by his circumstances. Instead, he was defined by the choices he made in those circumstances. He saw every moment as a second chance to live fully in the presence of God and in Leslie's love.

Let me briefly share the story of Lazarus. He was the brother of two women we meet a few times in the Gospels, Mary and Martha. They lived in Bethany, a village just east of Jerusalem. Once when Jesus was out of town, Lazarus got very sick. His sisters were very concerned and sent word to Jesus to ask Him to come to heal their brother. When Jesus got word, He delayed his trip by two days. When He and the disciples finally arrived in Bethany, Lazarus had been in his grave for four days. Martha and Mary met Jesus as He walked into town, and both of them poured out their grief, knowing that Jesus could have healed Lazarus like He had healed so many others.

In Jesus' conversation with Mary, He broke down: "When Jesus saw her weeping and saw the other people wailing with her, a deep anger welled up within him, and he was deeply troubled. 'Where have you put him?' he asked them. They told him, 'Lord, come and see.' Then Jesus wept" (John 11:33-35). Jesus was equally grieved at the loss of His friend and angry that death had done its worst.

When He arrived at the tomb, Jesus told the people to roll away the stone covering the entrance:

Martha protested, "Lord, he has been dead for four days. The smell will be terrible." Jesus responded, "Didn't I tell you that you would see God's glory if you believe?" So they rolled the stone aside. Then Jesus looked up to heaven and said, "Father, thank you for hearing me. You always hear me, but I said it out loud for the sake of all these people standing here, so that they will believe you sent me." Then Jesus shouted, "Lazarus, come out!" And the dead man came out, his hands and feet bound in graveclothes, his face wrapped in a headcloth. Jesus told them, "Unwrap him and let him go!" Many of the people who were with Mary believed in Jesus when they saw this happen" (vv. 39-45).

Thanks to Leslie Olson, I learned some important truths when I looked at this story through her eyes:

> Our timing isn't God's timing. Mary and Martha wanted Jesus to hurry back to heal their brother, but Jesus delayed. By the time He got there, Lazarus didn't need healing; he needed a resurrection! And that's what he got.

> God's agenda is always bigger than ours. When Jesus told the disciples they were going back to Bethany, they thought He had lost His mind. They had just been to Jerusalem where the religious authorities wanted to kill Him, but Jesus was willing to face any opposition to fulfill the Father's mission.

> Jesus can handle our fears and doubts. Mary and Martha were heartsick, and they told Him, "If only you had been here . . ."

Jesus wasn't defensive, and He wasn't harsh with the sisters. He let them express their emotions.

> Jesus' compassion was on full display. Most of us know the shortest verse in the Bible is "Jesus wept," but there's more to it than that. His deep love for Lazarus and the sisters and the horror of death produced the twin emotions of grief and anger. His anger wasn't out of control; it was the right response to something beautiful being ruined. A person created in the image of God, of unimaginable value, was being wasted by death.

> Jesus' delay was strategic. In that day, the Jews believed the soul could return to the body at any time for three days after death, so Jesus waited until the fourth day to come to Bethany. He wasn't going to let anyone think this was anything less than a glorious, shocking miracle. In *The Princess Bride*, Fezzik told Westley, "You've been mostly dead all day." Lazarus wasn't mostly dead. He was dead dead!

Jesus gave Lazarus a second chance at life, and he made the most of it.

TIME FOR A COMEBACK

I'm living on Lazarus time. My heart attack could have killed me, but God gave me a second chance at life. After the doctor put three stents in my heart, I experienced an irregular heartbeat from the medication. I had to stay in the hospital until it was under control, and one day, I wrote about my second chance on a whiteboard that was in my hospital room.

The realization that we have a second chance can come from all kinds of sources. For me, it was a health scare; others face the prospect of losing their marriage, their kids, their job, or their reputation. Like Lazarus, we receive a wakeup call, and like him, we often walk back into the light wearing graveclothes that need to be untied and unwrapped so we can live in our second-chance freedom. For all of us, the lesson is clear: Don't waste your Lazarus time!

For all of us, the lesson is clear: Don't waste your Lazarus time!

Alfred Nobel was the inventor of dynamite. Explosives, it seems, were in his blood: his father was an engineer who oversaw armaments factories and built underwater mines for Russia during the Crimean War. Alfred became known for developing new kinds of explosives, resulting in 355 patents for nitroglycerin detonators, blasting caps, smokeless gunpowder, and more. He owned nearly one hundred factories that made explosives and munitions, and became fabulously rich.

Alfred's brother Ludvig had a massive heart attack and died in 1888 while he was in France. A French newspaper got the name wrong and mistakenly reported that it was Alfred who died. The paper ran a scathing obituary, calling him a "merchant of death" who had grown rich by developing new ways to "mutilate and kill." According to one biographer, Alfred "became so obsessed with his posthumous reputation that he rewrote his last will, bequeathing most of his fortune to a cause upon which no future obituary writer would be able to cast aspersions."

Many people believe that's why "the dynamite king" had most of his estate dedicated to those who have made the world a better place through their work in physics, chemistry, medicine, literature, and peace. (A Nobel Prize for economics was added in 1968.)[18]

One of the most stunning comebacks in sports happened in Super Bowl LI between the New England Patriots and the Atlanta Falcons. The Patriots were led by Tom Brady, widely acknowledged as the GOAT, the greatest of all time, but the first half didn't go Brady's way. The Falcons scored touchdowns on three possessions and took a 21-3 lead into the locker room. In the third quarter, the Falcons scored again, extending the lead to 28-3. The game was, for all intents and purposes, over. No team had ever come back from such a deficit, but Brady and his team didn't give up. They scored a touchdown and a field goal, but with six minutes remaining in the game, they were still behind 28-12. The Falcons only had to run out the clock to enjoy their biggest win, but quarterback Matt Ryan was stripped of the ball, the Patriots scored two more times, and regulation time ended in a tie. In overtime, the Patriots won the coin toss and marched down the field for a touchdown. The comeback was complete.

The win was especially sweet for Brady. He had been suspended for four games at the start of the season for his role in a scandal called "Deflategate." He was accused of lowering the air pressure in footballs the Patriots used on offense to give himself and his receivers a better grip. He started the Super Bowl with something to prove, and he lived up to his goal. He completed 43 of 62 pass attempts for 466 yards and was named the game's MVP.

About a month after the game, I had dinner with Chris Long, a defensive end who played for the Patriots in the game. I asked the obvious question: "What was it like in the huddle and on the sidelines in the fourth quarter when the momentum turned in your favor?"

The look on his face told me he was instantly back in those pivotal minutes. He almost growled, "We could feel it! It was unbelievable! Even though we were behind by 25 and then 13 late in the game, we knew we were going to come back and win the game." Most of the game, the Patriots looked like losers, but they created their own second chance.

EVEN THEN

One of the most popular—and one of the most powerful—statements about our relationship with God is, "We have a God of second chances." For those who have blown it big time, this is a message of incredible hope, but let me be clear: I'd much rather celebrate a person's continued faithfulness and obedience, but I'm glad to cheer a comeback, too.

I'd much rather celebrate a person's continued faithfulness and obedience, but I'm glad to cheer a comeback, too.

When we've made a colossal mistake, or when we're so wounded we don't think life can go on, we often come to the mistaken conclusion that God is against us. Actually, God delights in turnarounds, in people who find the courage to climb back and start over . . . again . . . and again. Quite often, our suffering is self-inflicted, but we may experience pain from another sinning against us, a natural disaster, or pushback from people who don't appreciate our allegiance to Jesus. Whatever the source, God is with us, cheering us on.

Isaiah was a prophet just before the darkest days of Israel's history. The rulers and the people had drifted away from God to worship idols. The powerful Babylonians threatened the nation, and instead of trusting God, Israel's leaders tried to form an alliance with Egypt. They were making a series of colossal mistakes. God had tried to get their attention by bringing hardships on them, but they didn't listen. Isaiah still assured them:

> Though the Lord gave you adversity for food
>   and suffering for drink,
> he will still be with you to teach you.
>   You will see your teacher with your own eyes.

Your own ears will hear him.
Right behind you a voice will say,
"This is the way you should go,"
whether to the right or to the left.
Then you will destroy all your silver idols
and your precious gold images.
You will throw them out like filthy rags,
saying to them, "Good riddance!" (Isaiah 30:20-22)

God may whisper to us, or He may shout. Either way, it's never too late to repent and turn back to God, change our agenda, and make hard choices to get rid of the things that have distracted us. Every day is a second chance to start again.

WHAT DO YOU DO WITH A SECOND CHANCE?

Whatever you do, don't waste your second chance. God has given you an opportunity for a do-over. Don't ignore it, don't delay, and don't drift back into the excuses for remaining passive. I've noticed two main reasons people miss their second chances: self-pity and bitterness. For some, it just feels more comfortable to feel sorry for themselves and harbor resentment toward "those people" who let them down. Don't go there. And if you're there, get out as fast as you can!

In one of the most remarkable scenes in the Bible, we see King David in the wake of his sins of adultery and murder. Nathan went to him to tell him a story about a rich and powerful man who took a poor man's only lamb, killed it, and ate it. David was outraged and vowed that the rich man deserved to die! Nathan looked at the king and said, "You are that man!" David's heart broke, and he repented . . . but the consequences would be severe. Nathan told him, "The Lord has forgiven you, and you won't die for this sin. Nevertheless, because you have shown utter contempt for the word of the Lord by doing this, your child will die" (2 Samuel 12:13-14).

Soon, Bathsheba's baby got sick. David begged God to heal his child. He fasted, prayed, and lay on the ground for seven days. Still, the child eventually died. His advisors were afraid he would do something drastic if he heard the news, so they didn't tell him. But David figured it out. He asked, "Is the child dead?" They acknowledged the dreaded fact. Then, surprisingly, "David got up from the ground, washed himself, put on lotions, and changed his clothes. He went to the Tabernacle and worshiped the Lord. After that, he returned to the palace and was served food and ate" (v. 20). His team was surprised at his quick response, and he explained, "I fasted and wept while the child was alive, for I said, 'Perhaps the Lord will be gracious to me and let the child live.' But why should I fast when he is dead? Can I bring him back again? I will go to him one day, but he cannot return to me" (vv. 22-23). Soon, Bathsheba became pregnant again. This child was named Solomon and grew to be David's wise and prosperous successor.

Forgiveness, grief, and healing are often misunderstood. Some people try to get over their pain and shame too quickly, whether self-inflicted or caused by others, and they're surprised when the resentment and self-pity return. But others wait too long. They receive two things they value from remaining bitter: a clear, strong identity as "the one who was wronged" . . . and the energy that comes from hate. To take advantage of our second chances, we have to first be honest about the depths of the pain (and often deal with it in layers as we can handle it). Then we must find the courage to forgive the offender . . . "that person" who did us wrong, or ourselves for doing something self-destructive.

Lazarus made the most of his second chance. First, his sisters threw a party at their home in Bethany. As usual, Martha stayed in the kitchen, but Mary couldn't contain her joy and gratitude. She anointed Jesus' feet with a whole jar of expensive perfume. Lazarus's very presence at the dinner was a loud and powerful testimony of Jesus' love and power, so people came from all over to see him. "When all the people heard of Jesus' arrival, they flocked to see him and also to see Lazarus, the man Jesus had raised from the dead." But those who were pleasantly amazed weren't the only ones who were watching: "Then the leading priests decided to kill Lazarus, too, for it was because of him that many of the people had deserted them and believed in Jesus" (John 12:9-11). The mere fact that Lazarus was living and breathing shifted the allegiance of the people from the religious leaders to Jesus, and they became jealous. (I've always wondered what Lazarus thought when he learned that the religious leaders wanted to kill him. Did he think, *Hey, it wasn't that bad!* Or, *Here we go again!*)

Most of us think of Lazarus exclusively as the guy who was raised from the dead, but he used that second chance to have a huge impact in pointing people to Jesus. I don't think it's a stretch at all to conclude that his second chance was far more significant in God's kingdom than his life before his sickness and death.

When I was stuck in the hospital with an irregular heartbeat, one of the options was to shock my heart back into rhythm. That sounded pretty serious to me, but that wasn't the only warning. As I've mentioned, my doctor told me, "Rob, I'm not sure how much function you've lost from your heart attack. Some people have to significantly reduce their activity, and you could be one of them." Of course, I didn't want to slow down at all. I wanted to make the most of this fresh opportunity to live and love and serve. The heart attack was like a timeout to call the right play to win the game. I realized death wasn't some distant, ambiguous concept: it was going to happen . . . to me . . . so I rededicated myself to God because, more than ever, I wanted my life to count. Lazarus and I both received wakeup calls, and I appreciated every heartbeat, irregular or not. I had looked into the face of death, and the experience revolutionized me: at the same time, I had far more gratitude, far more peace, and far more drive than ever before. And no, thank God, I didn't lose any function that made me slow down. Sometimes at night I lie awake and listen to my heartbeat. I realize I have three pieces of metal in my heart, and these interventions are giving me plenty of second chances. I often get up in the morning and pray, "Thank You, God, that my heart is still beating. I'm so glad to serve You today!"

ALL OF US

Every person who has trusted in Jesus is living on Lazarus time because we've all been raised from the dead.

Every person who has trusted in Jesus is living on Lazarus time because we've all been raised from the dead. Don't believe me? Paul wrote to the Christians in and around Ephesus, "Once you were dead because of your disobedience and your many sins.

You used to live in sin, just like the rest of the world, obeying the devil—the commander of the powers in the unseen world" (Ephesians 2:1-2). Dead? Yes, dead, completely incapable of responding to God's goodness and grace. Lifeless, empty, and helpless. But just as Jesus didn't leave Lazarus in the tomb, God didn't leave us spiritually dead. Two of the most beautiful words in the Bible are in this passage: "But God." Paul goes on to tell us about the miracle of our resurrection:

> But God is so rich in mercy, and he loved us so much, that even though we were dead because of our sins, he gave us life when he raised Christ from the dead. (It is only by God's grace that you have been saved!) For he raised us from the dead along with Christ and seated us with him in the heavenly realms because we are united with Christ Jesus. (vv. 4-6)

You and I have come out of our tomb of spiritual death, raised by the power of our loving God! And God didn't pour out His grace and power reluctantly. He's thrilled with us! Paul amazes us:

> So God can point to us in all future ages as examples of the incredible wealth of his grace and kindness toward us, as shown in all he has done for us who are united with Christ Jesus. (v. 7)

Just to be sure we get the picture, Paul hammers the point that it's all by grace, not by our goodness, serving, or giving, and God's new creations aren't stuck in a closet somewhere—He considers us His masterpiece! When we realize we're God's treasure,

He becomes our treasure, and we want to give and love and serve with all our hearts—not to earn our acceptance with God but because He has already accepted us in the grace of Jesus.

> God saved you by his grace when you believed. And you can't take credit for this; it is a gift from God. Salvation is not a reward for the good things we have done, so none of us can boast about it. For we are God's masterpiece. He has created us anew in Christ Jesus, so we can do the good things he planned for us long ago. (vv. 8-10)

All of us have been given second chances. All of us are living on Lazarus time. The problem is that we're often afflicted with amnesia. We forget what God has done for us, to us, and in us. Sometimes I even forget that I've had a heart attack. Not long ago, I was at a buffet that served lobster and steak. Oh man, two things I love to eat! I started to fill my plate with heaping portions of both dishes, and then I remembered, *What am I doing? I've had a heart attack. I can't eat all of this!* So I asked for a single lobster claw and a small portion of steak.

Why do I restrict my eating habits to what's good for me, and why do Becca and I walk four miles every other day? It's not to show how disciplined I am. In one of my follow-up appointments with my doctor, he reminded me that the only motivation that has staying power is "the joy of the good," in other words, the magnificent benefits of keeping the change.

"The good" are the benefits of receiving God's grace to forgive, His power to transform, and His provision to equip us for every opportunity. David expressed a heart overflowing with gratitude:

Let all that I am praise the Lord;
> with my whole heart, I will praise his holy name.

Let all that I am praise the Lord;
> may I never forget the good things he does for me.

He forgives all my sins
> and heals all my diseases.

He redeems me from death
> and crowns me with love and tender mercies.

He fills my life with good things.
> My youth is renewed like the eagle's!
> (Psalm 103:1-5)

I (and I assume you too) need to regularly reflect on "the good things [God] does for me." David's list is enough to keep our hearts overflowing: God forgives, heals, redeems, crowns, and fills. We experience the first three when we've really messed up and need a second chance, and we experience the last two when we've made the most of that opportunity.

Are you telling people about the miracle of being raised from spiritual death to life? After my heart attack, I couldn't stop telling people that God had saved my life, and my excitement didn't just barely ooze from me—it erupted all day every day! And are you redirecting your resources to maximize your Lazarus-time impact? If not, you don't really appreciate it enough.

Find the rhythm of grace and realize the gift of time God has given you. Tell everyone you know that He has given you a new life and a second chance. Love the people God has put in your life like it's your last day with them. And enjoy God's beautiful creation, have fun, and experience God's delight all day every day.

You may have a dramatic story of a second chance, a near-death experience, or some other tragic event that caused you to peer into the abyss of death . . . or you may not. But all of us have danced on the precipice of hopeless, helpless, lonely, eternal separation from God, and He has snatched us back to become His beloved children. John almost shouts, "See how very much our Father loves us, for he calls us his children, and that is what we are!" (1 John 3:1) And that's what you are.

CONSIDER THIS:

1. What are some experiences that shake people to the core and make them feel that life is hopeless?

2. Who do you know who has taken advantage of a second chance? Describe what happened and the person's response.

3. What are some reasons self-pity and bitterness seem so attractive to a lot of people? What's the upside of remaining stuck there? What's the downside?

4. Imagine being Lazarus when he learned that the religious leaders had decided to kill him. How do you think you would've responded to that news?

5. Look again at Ephesians 2:1-10. How does Paul describe our death and resurrection? What points in this passage give you a deep sense of gratitude?

6. Take some time to read the first verses of Psalm 103 at the end of the chapter and put them in your own words. What difference would it (or does it) make to remember these gifts from God?

7. What are some specific ways you can take advantage of your Lazarus time?

CHAPTER 6

◢ "I STILL . . ."

By perseverance the snail reached the ark.

—Charles Spurgeon

Before I was released from the hospital after my heart attack, my doctor prepared to give me the speech he always gives people who experience the same event. As he started, he realized it wasn't necessary. I'd already been eating a healthy diet, exercising, and staying on top of my cholesterol and other important numbers, so he deviated from his canned speech and said, "Rob, keep doing what you've been doing. It's worked for you before, so don't stop now." That was good to hear. A few days after my discharge from the hospital, I went to my first cardiac rehab appointment. When I looked around, I felt totally out of place—I was the skinniest, youngest person in the room. The physician's assistant gathered all of us for a class, and she explained all the changes we would need to make to take better care of our hearts. For each one, I could say, "Check." "Already doing that." "No problem."

For most of the people in the room, the changes would be monumental and difficult, but I felt like I was taking a test that I'd already aced. I was *still* going to eat more salmon and less red meat. I was *still* going to eat smaller portions and share desserts with Becca. We were *still* going to walk four miles every other day.

In fact, if Becca's not with me and I'm served a dessert, I cut it in half and give the other half back to the waiter, or I leave it on the plate so it can be thrown away. When I get a chicken sandwich, I take the meat out and throw the bun in the garbage. Why? Because bread is one of the chief culprits of weight gain. I've even learned to read the labels of packets of sauce so I can pick the one with fewer calories—and in case you didn't know, some have far more than others! Establishing new habits takes some work, no doubt, but I'd already done that. Now, keeping those habits requires rituals and reminders.

One of the turning points for most of us is when we've reached our goal: when we're out of debt, when we've lost the weight, when we're home for dinner four nights a week, when our marriages are more affirming, when we've been clean and sober for a year, and on and on. After those achievements, it's easy to assume we can take some liberties. Don't do it! It's critical to hold to our convictions. "I still manage my money wisely." "I still watch what I eat and how often I exercise." "I still need to guard my time with my family." "I still need to have a date with my spouse every week and resolve differences before they become volcanic explosions." "I still need to go to meetings and say 'no' to people who offer me a drink or drugs." (You can add others that are important to you.)

STAYING FOCUSED

People who don't have an "I still" mentality can fall back into old habits pretty quickly. In addition to diet and exercise, let me identify just a few ways a rock-solid commitment makes a difference.

People who don't have an "I still" mentality can fall back into old habits pretty quickly.

Finances

Dave Ramsey is a financial expert who has helped tens of thousands of people get out of debt and stay out. I talked to a couple who used his envelope system to assign particular amounts of monthly income to paying off debt, spending, saving, and giving. It had been twenty years since they became "debt free," but they still use the same system. It worked for them when they were in trouble, and it still works for them now.

Addictions

I know a man whose life was wrecked by alcohol when he was young. He lost his wife and kids, and he almost lost his business. Someone took him to an AA meeting, and he got his first chip. He recently celebrated twenty-five years of sobriety. He has been reunited with his wife and rebuilt trust with his children, and he has a clear mind to operate this business . . . but he still goes to two AA meetings every week. I asked him about that, and he smiled and said, "Rob, I'm not worried about drinking again, but I love the guys in our meetings. I want to be there for them because I remember how important it was that people stepped up for me. That's why I still go."

Career

Several years ago, our church invited Walter Bond to speak to our men's ministry. Walter played in the NBA for three seasons, but by his own admission, he wasn't a supremely ~~gifted athlete.~~ He was able to make a career in professional basketball because he didn't take any days off from his tenacious commitment to do the little things well. Even when he was tired, and even when he wasn't playing many minutes, he still went to the gym to work on the fundamentals. In games, he didn't go for the glory of launching three-point shots from the perimeter; he still went into the paint to rebound among the enormous, sweaty guys who were trying their best to take the ball away from him. Even though teammates would sometimes change plays, he still ran plays exactly the way the coach set them up. He was determined that nobody was going to hustle more, and nobody was going to practice more. He told our men, "I had a career in the NBA because I was committed to the fundamentals of the game. I was disciplined. I never stopped doing the things that helped me to be the best I could be. No one could out-execute me." That was his version of an "I still" declaration.

Parenting

I've watched some parents experience "discipline fatigue" and stop correcting their kids' bad behavior. I know how exhausted parents can be, and it's much easier to deal with behavior problems by ignoring them and hoping they'll change or letting the television become the surrogate parent. Don't get me wrong: I'm not against hope, and sometimes an iPad game or video is a good solution, but not if the child learns that misbehavior is normal and acceptable. I'm sure different parents claim that children "are the worst" at various ages, but for me, it was when our son Logan was a toddler. He was strong willed . . . incredibly strong willed! He carried the terrible twos with him the next couple of years. I remember one day when we put him in a time out, he wouldn't stay there. It may have looked comical to somebody who had a secret camera, but it wasn't funny to me. I was exasperated with that little boy! I sat in a chair with my hand on him to keep him in his timeout spot. Becca looked at me and said, "Really?"

I told her, "Whatever it takes."

On one of Logan's birthdays, we took him and a bunch of his friends to Chuck E. Cheese. I knew it would be chaos, but it was a birthday party, so I was all in! At some point in the middle of pizza and the incredibly nasty little plastic balls the kids jumped into, I realized the tickets the kids had earned would take hours to redeem. I came up with a plan. I asked the guy working there, "Do we have enough tickets for all ten boys to have a pencil and a little car?" He looked at my wad of tickets and nodded. I called the kids to me and told them they were all getting the same thing, but Logan whined, "I don't like that! I don't want that!"

I told him, "Son, that's the way it's going to work." He complained again, so I said, "That's fine. If you don't want yours, you won't get them." He complained—long and loud—all the way home. When we turned into the driveway, I explained, "Son, let this be a lesson for you. When you complain and demand things, you just might not get them." I had unknowingly tapped into a parenting strategy a friend of mine used when his kids were little: "Whatever you whine for, you automatically don't get." He told me that this statement made an enormous difference in his children, and not coincidentally, in his peace of mind, but he had to be consistent.

Spiritual life

In my spiritual life, I still use a Bible study method that has been meaningful to me for many years: SOAP stands for Scripture, Observation, Application, and Prayer. So, when I read the Bible, I take a few minutes to notice "who, what, when, where, and how," I find a specific way I can apply the truth I've learned, and I ask God to make it real in my life. In a similar way, when our boys went to Bible college, I encouraged them to keep their hearts soft by going to the altar every time the chapel message meant something to them.

Many times people claim they're too busy to respond to a challenging sermon, or they make other excuses to avoid wrestling with God and their hearts. I want them to listen to God, avoid procrastinating, have a responsive heart, and choose to obey immediately.

Forgiving those who offend us

When people hurt me, I still forgive. Peter asked Jesus, "Lord, how often should I forgive someone who sins against me? Seven times?" I'm sure that seemed extravagant to Peter, but Jesus set Peter's sights a little higher: "No, not seven times, but seventy times seven!" (Matthew 18:21-22)

I had dinner with the leader of an inner-city ministry in San Francisco, and at the end of our time together, he pushed back from the table and told me, "Rob, you've restored my faith in pastors of big churches." I had no idea how he drew that conclusion from our conversation, so I asked him to explain. He said, "You still forgive, you still love, you still have hope, you still experience joy. You're still in awe of who God is and what He's doing in your life!"

I've learned to forgive more fully and more quickly for two reasons: First, when I don't forgive, hurt turns to anger, which turns to resentment, which becomes the cancer of bitterness. At that point the disease spreads, and I become a self-absorbed husband, a demanding dad, and an angry leader . . . so I forgive the offender to get out of that destructive cycle. And second, when I'm totally amazed at the fact that God sent Jesus to pay the price to forgive me, how can I withhold forgiveness from people who have offended me?

Over the course of my career as a pastor, I've experienced my fair share of misunderstandings that led to suspicion and distance, and I had to address the hurt on both sides in those situations. On two occasions, I've also had the shock of discovering that people had mismanaged church finances. Both times, those people created a world of trouble. Again, we had very frank conversations and God brought us through, and He gave me the grace to forgive them. Today, if I saw them, I'd give them both a big hug. No matter what someone does to me, I still forgive because resentment is so corrosive to me, and God has filled my heart with enough grace for it to overflow into the lives of others.

Generosity

No matter what happens, Becca and I are committed to still give to the Lord and His cause. In 2020, before Covid changed our world (at least for a few years), we made a pledge to give the largest amount we'd ever given to missions through our church ministry called Kingdom Builders. A few months later, the pandemic was in full swing, churches had gone online, and the economic outlook was very uncertain. At the end of the year when our church has our annual Miracle Offering, Becca and I had the money to meet our pledge. However, when we looked at the chaos in our world, we agreed that *just in case* things went downhill really badly, we would hold onto that money for a while. That night, neither of us could sleep. The next morning, I told

Becca, "I think we bought into the lie of 'just in case.' God has blessed us, and we're still obedient to the voice of God, whatever the circumstances. I still want to give this money, and I still want to give it now." She wholeheartedly agreed.

> I told our church the story of our wrestling with giving because we'd listened to the lie of "just in case," and something amazing happened. Until that moment, a lot of people had been hesitant to give generously due to the uncertainty of the times. When they heard our story, it unleashed a wave of generosity, and they gave more than ever before. We rose up as individuals and as a church, saying, "God has been so generous. I'll still trust Him and be obedient to be generous with what He has put in my hands. We refuse to listen to the lie of 'just in case.'"

I'm sure there are many other ways to apply an "I still" tenacity, but these at least provide a few examples of the commitment and the benefits.

WARNING FLAGS

A change in circumstances—a move, a promotion, a new baby, children graduating from high school or college, a death in the family, or a hundred other factors, both positive and negative—can interrupt our healthy rhythms. I've learned that I need to adapt to any new circumstances, but I don't waver on my convictions. I still do what I need to do to follow through with my commitments. For instance, living in Minnesota in the winter makes it hard to go for walks. Do Becca and I just bag our commitment for the eleven months of cold weather there? (Well, maybe not eleven, but you get the point.) No way. We find ways to adapt. We go to the mall to walk, or we use the treadmill in the basement. And we walk when we're on vacation in warmer locations. No matter what, we still get our walking in.

I've learned that I need to adapt to any new circumstances, but I don't waver on my convictions.

If we're not careful, "I still" becomes "I used to." If we hear ourselves saying that, it's a yellow flag (and maybe a red one) warning us to take a long look at our commitments. When we stop our "I still," we're either already using excuses or we're getting ready to use them. Let me offer some time-tested, practical advice to keep the change.

Start with an achievable goal.

Dave Ramsey advises people in debt to pay off the smallest ones first and work their way up to the daunting ones. He calls it "the debt snowball method":

> You pay off debt in order of smallest to largest, gaining momentum as you knock out each remaining balance. When the smallest debt is paid in full, you roll the minimum payment you were making on that debt into the next-smallest debt payment.

Here's how it works:

Step 1: List your debts from smallest to largest regardless of interest rate.

Step 2: Make minimum payments on all your debts except the smallest.

Step 3: Pay as much as possible on your smallest debt.

Step 4: Repeat until each debt is paid in full.[19]

Don't try to change your entire world all at once.
Yes, I know that some of us need to make some global, sweeping changes, but even then, we need to establish priorities. If the problem is critical, like a major health concern, start with two or three that are absolutely necessary, but most of us need to focus on one at a time so we can see success and keep going. When we attempt too many changes at the same time, it's easy to feel overwhelmed and give up on all of them.

Measure your new behavior, not the outcome.
Yes, you want a specific result from your new habit, but it's wise to spend more mental energy on establishing the habit and let the outcome take care of itself. For instance, many people have trouble losing weight. Their focus needs to be on their diet and exercise, not the number on the scale every morning.

Pay attention to the water where you swim.
In an article on the reasons why attempts to create new habits often fail, psychologist James Clear observes that our surroundings make the difference in success or failure:

I have never seen a person consistently stick to positive habits in a negative environment. You can frame this statement in many different ways:

> It is nearly impossible to eat healthy all of the time if you are constantly surrounded by unhealthy food.

> It is nearly impossible to remain positive all of the time if you are constantly surrounded by negative people.

> It is nearly impossible to focus on a single task if you are constantly bombarded with text messages, notifications, emails, questions, and other digital distractions.

> It is nearly impossible to not drink if you are constantly surrounded by alcohol.

And so on.

We rarely admit it (or even realize it), but our behaviors are often a simple response to the environment we find ourselves in. In fact, you can assume that the lifestyle you have today (all of your habits) is largely a product of the environment you live in each day. The single biggest change that will make a new habit easier is performing it in an environment that is designed to make that habit succeed.[20]

The goal of keeping the change isn't to impress anyone that we've conquered the highest mountain without all the necessary gear. The goal is to start well, bite off just enough to make real progress, and gradually add more hills to climb—unless, of course, the change needs to be critical. In those cases, gradual improvement won't do. Drastic action is necessary.

BEYOND DISCIPLINE

In the world of addiction recovery, some people try to overcome their problem and maintain abstinence by sheer force of their wills. They call it "white knuckling," which refers to a high level of anxiety demonstrated by a tightly clinched fist. For all the changes we need to make and keep, discipline is only part of the equation. Two other elements are even more important: conviction and being yielded to God. *Conviction* is a strongly held belief. It's far more than an idea or an opinion; it's a position that a concept is true and necessary. I think most people have lots of opinions but far fewer convictions—about God, their purpose, their values, or anything else. If we have only an opinion that we need to keep a particular change, we may not last long in our discipline. But if we have a conviction, we'll have more staying power. Convictions are often the result of either careful study or a sudden crisis. We may examine a truth or a concept that's important to us, and we settle on what seems right. But quite often, our convictions are the product of discontent, heartbreak, or tragedy. We look in the mirror, hear a diagnosis, look into a coffin, watch our house burn to the ground, see our prodigal child in jail, get a notice of bankruptcy, or experience some other soul-churning event. Convictions, no matter the source, have lasting power.

We *yield* our hearts, our resources, our relationships, and our futures to Him because we trust in our good and great God.

But convictions can be nothing more than self-effort. We are people who belong to the Creator, Savior, and King. Everything we are, everything we have, and everything we do find their ultimate meaning only in Him. Those who resist submitting to the authority of God haven't yet grasped the wonder of His love. We *yield* our hearts, our resources, our relationships, and our futures to Him because we trust in our good and great God. At the pivotal point in his letter to the Romans, Paul captured the essence of what it means to yield to God: "Therefore, I urge you, brothers and sisters, in view of God's mercy, to offer your bodies as a living sacrifice, holy and pleasing to God—this is your true and proper worship. Do not conform to the pattern of this world, but be transformed by the renewing of your mind. Then you will be able to test and approve what God's will is—his good, pleasing and perfect will" (Romans 12:1-2 NIV).

As always, Paul points us to God's grace. Our willingness to yield ("to offer your bodies as a living sacrifice") is the reasonable response to the wonders of grace he has described in the first eleven chapters. Grace and mercy are closely related. Mercy means God doesn't give us the punishment we deserve for our sins; grace means that and more: that God forgives us, adopts us, cherishes us, fills us, and equips us to make a difference in our world. Living for God is "true and proper," that is, a heartfelt response to what He has done for us. His truth revolutionizes how we think, shaping our convictions, and transforming our values. We no longer pursue the idols of success, pleasure, and approval. If God gives us these things, that's fine—we hold them loosely. But if not, we're content in Him. As our convictions grow, we live an "upside-down" life, humbling ourselves, serving gladly, and giving generously . . . not because we have to, but because we want to.

Some people assume that being yielded to God implies they obey because they're afraid of what He might do if they disobey, but as John reminds us, "[God's] love has no fear, because perfect love expels all fear. If we are afraid, it is for fear of punishment, and this shows that we have not fully experienced his perfect love" (1 John 4:18).

Is discipline important? Yes, of course, but it's not enough. Are convictions essential? Certainly, but they might leave God out of the picture. Having a heart softened by grace makes us happy and determined to follow Jesus wherever He leads us. Every day, I still need to experience the wonder of His extravagant love.

Suffering produces perseverance; perseverance, character; and character, hope." [Paul] lists hope at the end, instead of where I would normally expect it, at the beginning, as the fuel that keeps a person going. No, hope emerges from the struggle, a byproduct of faithfulness.

Philip Yancey

CONSIDER THIS:

1. What are some habits that have become so ingrained in the rhythm of your life that you still do them no matter what's going on? What impact do these habits have on you, your relationships, and your influence on other people?

2. Which of the brief illustrations of commitments (finances, career, parenting, etc.) is an area of strength? Which one needs some attention? What needs to happen in them?

3. When have you experienced significant changes in your circumstances (a move, a promotion, death of a loved one, etc.)? Did you keep your convictions and your healthy habits during that season of change? Why or why not?

4. Look again at Romans 12:1-2. How does Paul encourage us to keep the change? What happens when someone relies on sheer willpower, self-discipline, to keep a change?

5. Are your core convictions the product of study and reflection, or your experiences in a crisis? Explain your answer.

6. How do the love, kindness, and power of God invite us to yield our hearts and our agendas to Him?

7. On a scale of 0 (not in the least) to 10 (all day every day), how much are you yielded to God? Explain your answer. What do you need to respond to His gracious invitation?

CHAPTER 7

◢ IT'S ALL IN YOUR HEAD

As you begin changing your thinking, start immediately to change your behavior. Begin to act the part of the person you would like to become. Take action on your behavior. Too many people want to feel, then take action. This never works.

— *John Maxwell*

In a chapel service when I was in Bible college, the speaker told the story of "The Eagle Who Lived Like a Chicken." It goes like this: Two eagles built a nest on a mountainside, and the female laid four eggs. One day before they hatched, an earthquake shook the nest, and one of the eggs rolled down the mountain into a chicken farm. The egg was much bigger than the other eggs, but the chickens treated it like one of their own. When the egg hatched, the eagle chick looked around and saw only chickens, so he assumed that he was a chicken, too. One day the eaglet saw a majestic eagle soaring in the sky, and he told the chickens that he wanted to fly like that. The chickens laughed at him and said, "You can't fly! You're just a chicken!" As the eaglet and the chicks grew, they imitated the adult chickens on the farm. After a while, the eagle stopped looking up to marvel at the eagles he saw flying high above the farm. He lived like a chicken ... and he died like a chicken. I remember the chapel speaker shouting, "I'm an eagle, not a chicken!" Then he turned to all of us listening to him, and he told us, "And you . . . you are an eagle, not a chicken! You were made to soar above the earth, not peck around in the dirt! Be who God created you to be!" The story may be only a children's fable, but it has a profound message for each of us: We become who we believe we are.

After God miraculously freed his people from slavery in Egypt, Moses planned to take them to the Promised Land. As a good leader, Moses was into strategic planning. He picked twelve men as scouts to go ahead into Canaan. He told them, "Go north through the Negev into the hill country. See what the land is like, and find out whether the people living there are strong or weak, few or many. See what kind of land they live in. Is it good or bad? Do their towns have walls, or are they unprotected like open camps? Is the soil fertile or poor? Are there many trees? Do your best to bring back samples of the crops you see" (Numbers 13:17-20).

The men found the land to be abundant. After their forty-day reconnaissance, they brought back pomegranates, figs, and a huge cluster of grapes. They reported, "We entered the land you sent us to explore, and it is indeed a bountiful country—a land flowing with milk and honey. Here is the kind of fruit it produces. But the people living there are powerful, and their towns are large and fortified. We even saw giants there, the descendants of Anak!" (vv. 27-28)

Most of the spies were afraid to attack the people they'd seen . . . and to the fearful spies, those people seemed like monsters! Caleb, one of two of the spies who had a different opinion, told Moses and the people who had gathered to listen to the report,

"Let's go at once to take the land. We can certainly conquer it!" (v. 30)

Did Caleb's courage change the minds of the ten who were afraid? Did he put steel in their souls? Not exactly. "But the other men who had explored the land with him disagreed. 'We can't go up against them! They are stronger than we are!'"

To gain some allies, the doubters tried to convince the people that they were right to be so afraid—and that Caleb had lost his mind! "So they spread this bad report about the land among the Israelites: 'The land we traveled through and explored will devour anyone who goes to live there. All the people we saw were huge. We even saw giants there, the descendants of Anak. Next to them we felt like grasshoppers, and that's what they thought, too!'" (vv. 31-33)

"We felt like grasshoppers." What a self-concept! They had seen exactly the same things Caleb had seen, but they had come to a completely opposite set of beliefs.

"We felt like grasshoppers." What a self-concept!

A few years ago, nine other pastors and I were scheduled to have a meeting with Bill Bright, the founder and president of CRU, an international parachurch evangelistic ministry. Dr. Bright was (and still is, even years after his death) a legend in Christian history. He launched ministries on hundreds of college campuses in America and sent thousands of missionaries around the world. His team created the *Jesus* film based on the Gospel of

Luke, which has been translated into over 1,800 languages and dialects and shown to over three billion people. At the time, his health was failing, so instead of joining us in person, we stood in his office while he called us from his home. As we talked to him, I glanced around the room to see what mementos were meaningful to him. On his desk was a little sign that said, "I am not a grasshopper."

Instantly, I thought, *This is going to preach!* I came back home and prepared a message with that title. I told the story about the spies, and I contrasted the self-evaluation of Caleb (and Joshua, too) with the ten doubters. I explained, "Many of you are limiting yourself in your own mind. God is speaking to you like Caleb spoke to Moses and the people: 'You're a possessor. You're an overcomer. You're a giant-killer. A land flowing with milk and honey is yours for the taking, but you've told yourself you're nothing more than a grasshopper. Your self-talk is holding you back. Your limitations are all in your head."

This isn't "the power of positive thinking," it's not magic, and it's not hyper-spiritual. It's far more than *Saturday Night Live's* Stuart Smalley repeating, "I'm good enough, I'm smart enough, and doggone it, people like me!" That's hopeful (and maybe delusional) thinking, not biblical thinking. We need to align our thoughts with the truths of the Bible about who we are and with the promises of God about what He has called us to do. Remember, God sees you and me as His masterpiece. We have been adopted into God's family and filled with the power of the Holy Spirit. We're partners with God in the family business of drawing people to faith in Christ and advancing His kingdom of kindness, grace, righteousness, and justice. Nothing less than that.

THE GLORY AND THE FIGHT

Two New Testament passages give more substance to the concept of good and godly self-talk. In his letter to the Philippians, Paul promises they will experience more peace than they ever thought possible as they pray with thanksgiving, and he expands on his advice:

> And now, dear brothers and sisters, one final thing. Fix your thoughts on what is true, and honorable, and right, and pure, and lovely, and admirable. Think about things that are excellent and worthy of praise. Keep putting into practice all you learned and received from me—everything you heard from me and saw me doing. Then the God of peace will be with you." (Philippians 4:8-9)

Earlier in the letter, Paul describes Jesus in one of the most powerful and beautiful passages in the Bible. He says that Jesus is equal with God, but He "gave up his divine privileges," "took the humble position of a slave," and "humbled himself in obedience to God and died a criminal's death on a cross." But God raised Him from the tomb and "elevated him to the place of highest honor," where He would receive praise and adoration for all eternity (Philippians 2:6-11). Now, back to chapter four: Paul is saying, "Do you want to fix your thoughts on what's true? Start and end with Jesus, who is The Truth. And Jesus is honorable, right, pure, lovely, and admirable. Think about Him—a lot—and the rest of your mental energies will be more encouraging and productive."

But Paul was a practical pastor, and he knew how hard it is to keep our thoughts riveted on things that nourish us instead of poisoning us. In his last letter to the Corinthians, he compared our mental fight to siege warfare: "We are human, but we don't wage war as humans do. We use God's mighty weapons, not worldly weapons, to knock down the strongholds of human reasoning and to destroy false arguments. We destroy every proud obstacle that keeps people from knowing God. We capture their rebellious thoughts and teach them to obey Christ" (2 Corinthians 10:3-5).

We can't stop all the negative, self-defeating, condemning, prideful, jealous, ugly thoughts that come into our heads, but we can keep them from renting space there.

We can't stop all the negative, self-defeating, condemning, prideful, jealous, ugly thoughts that come into our heads, but we can keep them from renting space there. As the old saying goes, "You can't stop birds from flying over your head, but you can keep them from building a nest in your hair."

Over the years, I've used a simple but effective technique to combat unworthy thoughts. First I have to notice them, which isn't as easy as it sounds. Some of the evil, crushing, shameful thoughts that come into our minds sound a lot like our own voices, such as, "I'm such an idiot!" Now, if the thought was, "Satan says I'm an idiot," we'd identify it as foreign a lot more quickly, but using "I" makes it more sinister and powerful. When I notice and name these thoughts, I imagine using a piece of black paper to blot out the thought, and I knock it out of my mind, replacing it with something good, right, and true. If it comes back, I put the black paper over it again and knock it out of my thoughts. A siege is a long, patient form of combat, and that's the way we need to destroy the pride, self-pity, resentment, and comparison that often plague our thought-life.

A CLOSER LOOK

Have you ever taken stock of what goes on in your mind all day every day? We might categorize our destructive self-talk in three ways:

Pitiful me
"I can't."
"I have no idea what to do."
"Nobody really cares for me."

"Everybody is smarter than me, better looking than me, funnier than me."

"I'm a loser."

"I'm such a fool."

Powerful me

"I have to be on top, no matter what."

"If they don't agree with me and follow me, I'll bury them."

"He's nothing without me."

"It's not my fault."

"She can't make it without me."

"He's an incompetent fool."

Anxious and overly responsible me

"If I don't step in to help, who will?"

"Even if no one else comes through for him, I will."

"Nobody appreciates all I do for him."

"If she would only do what I tell her to do."

"I'm the only one they can trust."

"They can't find their way out of a wet paper bag without me."

These statements aren't isolated, stand-alone self-analysis. When one of them enters our minds, it's usually followed by a wave of self-condemnation or self-righteousness—and sometimes both. And they happen to all of us to some extent. When I was a young pastor, I felt less secure. When I was preaching and people looked at me like they were zombies, I went into "a death spiral" of self-doubt: *Why did I pick this passage? Why don't they like what I said? Why don't they like me? Why am I a pastor anyway?* I envisioned myself as the pilot of a fighter plane who was suffering from vertigo! I'm spinning down toward the ground, and all I can think is, *Pull up! Pull up! You're going to crash!* All of this happened while I was preaching, making eye contact, and trying my best to land the plane. Sometimes I felt so disconnected from the people that I stopped and found a place in the notes that I knew would hit home with them, and I jumped to that part of the message. I'd do anything to get out of the death spiral!

When we read about Elijah the prophet, we might be amazed that after one of the most dramatic victories the world has ever seen—the day Elijah called down fire from heaven and single-handedly (along with God) defeated the prophets of Baal on Mount Carmel—he had his own death spiral of depression and ran away from his mission. But I'm not at all surprised. The same thing often happens to me. On Mondays, I often have to fight thoughts like, *The sermon was terrible. Nobody's life was changed. My life doesn't matter. I should have become an entrepreneur or a salesman . . . or anything but a pastor.* I'd like to say I'm beyond this now, but these thoughts still blast me on many Mondays. I've learned that it's not a good idea for me to try to make major decisions on Mondays because I'm too preoccupied with beating myself to a pulp.

My friend Craig Groeschel, who is one of the most dynamic pastors in the country, told me that sometimes in the past when he got up to preach, he was filled with so much anxiety that he had to stop at the side of the stage and tell himself, *Look, God called you. He knew what He was doing. It's not about you, it's about Him. Now go up there and be the pastor God has called you to be.* I can't tell you how much that has encouraged me. I thought I was the only one! I've learned to follow Craig's example of stopping on the way to the stage to give myself a good talking to.

The problem isn't limited to pastors. When you invite friends over for dinner, you might think, *I don't know why I fixed this dish. It's going to be terrible. I'm so ashamed, and they haven't even arrived yet.*

Or after you put your children to bed, you think, *They're going to need counseling to fix what I've broken. I just hope they don't need an asylum. I'm the worst parent in the world.*

Or before a meeting with your boss, you think, *What if he's in his normal bad mood and he takes it out on me? He'll find something wrong with everything I've done and plan to do. This is going to be a disaster.*

Or almost anytime, you might hear the voice of a critical parent, *You can't do anything right. Why can't you be like your sister?*

Or if you've had stress in your marriage, you might remember a single sentence you can't get out of your mind: *My mother told me not to marry you because you're such a loser!*

Or before you post something on social media, you think, *This is really going to impress people.* But after you post it, you immediately draw a very different conclusion: *I'm so stupid! Why did I think that was a good idea?*

In fact, let me interject some observations my son Logan and others have made about the blessing and the curse of social media. When people use it wisely, it enables them to stay in touch with each other and communicate love, joy, and information about their lives. But in our intensely polarized culture, social media has become the weapon of choice for millions of people who are determined to win the war of ideas at all costs. Almost two thousand years ago, James, Jesus' half-brother, made an observation that's always accurate: "The tongue is a small thing that makes grand speeches. But a tiny spark can set a great forest on fire. And among all the parts of the body, the tongue is a flame of fire. It is a whole world of wickedness, corrupting your entire body. It can set your whole life on fire, for it is set on fire by hell itself" (James 3:5-6). Today, the social media landscape is a dry, parched forest, and a lot of people are setting it on fire!

The fact that we can post comments without seeing the look in another person's eyes has caused many people to have two separate identities: they're fierce lions online and meek kittens in person. But others have let their fierce side become dominant in every interaction, in person or online.

In the flames of attacks and defense of our positions, we look for posts, likes, and retweets to confirm our ideas, and we ignore or blast anyone who has a different point of view. This is called "confirmation bias," and it leaves us more entrenched and even angrier than before. In this environment, reasoned reflection is overwhelmed by instant and furious reactions, and truth is lost in snarky posts. William Barclay was a Scottish minister and theologian. Decades before social media became a thing, he wrote, "There is nothing so impossible to kill as a rumour; there is nothing so impossible to obliterate as an idle and malignant story. Let a man [or woman] before he speaks, remember that once a word is spoken it is gone from his control; and let him think before he speaks because, although he cannot get it back, he will most certainly answer for it."[21] Someday, we will all give an account to God for the words we've spoken, written, liked, and retweeted.

Many of today's experts agree with Barclay. Arthur Brooks is the president of the American Enterprise Institute, a conservative think tank, and a columnist for *The Atlantic*. He observes that many of our debates about ideas don't change anyone's mind:

The way that people tend to argue today, particularly online, makes things worse. Disagreements can feel like a war in which the fighters dig trenches on either side of any issue and launch their beliefs back and forth like grenades. You wouldn't blame anyone involved for feeling as if they're under fire, and no one is likely to change their mind when they're being attacked. These sorts of fights might give everyone involved some short-term satisfaction—*they deserve it because I am right and they are evil!*—but odds are that neither camp is having any effect on the other; on the contrary, the attacks make opponents dig in deeper. If you want a chance at changing minds, you need a new strategy: Stop using your values as a weapon, and start offering them as a gift.[22]

We can implement at least three specific steps as antidotes to online escalation of anger: First, after writing a comment, wait an hour before posting it—you may want to rephrase it, or you may realize that it's not wise to send it at all. Second, instead of assuming people on the other side are stupid and evil, seek to understand them, invite deeper dialogue, forgive, keep your cool, and find at least one thing you can agree on. And finally, realize there are real people reading your posts, so treat them with respect, dignity, and love . . . the way you want to be treated.[23]

Our self-destructive thoughts aren't limited to a few times and places—we take them with us wherever we go! I'm sure you have your own variations. You might say that we're infinitely creative in injecting into our minds a noxious cloud of self-doubt, self-condemnation, and self-loathing. A friend of mine says that when he was a boy and worked on a toy, a game, or any project, his father stood over him saying, "You're going to mess it up! Can't you do it right?" He's now in his 50s, and he has to overcome that loud, recurring voice every time he does any work around his house. His dad has been dead for twenty years, but his voice is still alive in my friend's head. The voice of our parents is incredibly powerful, and of course, it's quite often a mixed voice of affirmation and condemnation. Many of us, however, only remember the words of criticism, and these are branded on our souls.

The toxic voice in our minds takes many forms. One of the most powerful is comparison. We look around at other people to see how we measure up. If we see someone who has really messed up, we feel superior, but far more often, we notice another person's success or beauty or car or vacation or obedient children and conclude, *I'm such a loser. I've really messed up my life. Nothing ever works out for me.* And we experience our own version of the death spiral. We might wonder, *Why did I become a teacher instead of a hedge fund manager? I blew my career and my life!* A form that's closely associated with comparison is "shoulds." We feel deficient, so we think, *I should be a better mother (or father). I should be smarter. I should be more flexible. I should be more attractive. I should be more popular.* These are classic dissatisfiers, which are like sandpaper eroding any sense of gratitude, peace, and joy.

As a pastor, I'm an authority figure . . . whether I like or not. Sometimes, people see me as a stand-in for one of their parents. Psychologists call this *transference.* Years ago a woman in our church was very upset with me. I talked to her a couple of times, but these attempts didn't resolve anything. In fact, it got worse. I scheduled a time for the two of us to talk to a counselor, who I hoped could clear the air. When we sat down, the counselor asked me to express my heart to the woman. I told her, "We love you. We want the very best for you. We're thrilled that you want to be part of our church."

The counselor turned to her and said, "Now, what did you hear from Pastor Rob?"

She snarled, "He said I'm a loser, I'm worthless, and he doesn't want me in his church!"

I was stunned. I turned to the counselor and asked if I'd said anything like that. He would have laughed at me if the situation hadn't been so serious. He told me, "No, you didn't. Please tell her again what you said before." I did, and she responded in exactly the same way. I tried to dive back in to reassure her, but the problem wasn't that I had been unclear the first time . . . or the second. The problem was that she could only hear the messages of her parents, and she effectively translated everything I said into their harsh, vicious, hateful words. She had transferred her perceptions and her emotions about her parents onto me. She didn't hear love and affirmation; she heard only bitter condemnation.

I understand that the wiring in our brains is developed very early in our lives, and many of our reactions as adults are the result of what happened years before. When emotionally fragile people feel threatened, they experience an "amygdala hijacking," which is the chemical reaction in that small part of the brain that instantly kicks in the fight-or-flight response. It's so powerful and so overwhelming that it shuts down the front part of the brain where we reason things out. In other words, we react defensively before we can think. Has that ever happened to you? Has it happened in your relationships with family members, friends, and colleagues? Of course it has.

Is it possible to change our brains? In recent years, science has learned that the brain has the amazing characteristic of *plasticity*—the ability to be shaped. In his book about childhood trauma, Dr. Bessel Van Der Kolk explains, "The human brain is a social organ that is shaped by experience, and that is shaped in order to respond to the experience that you're having. So particularly earlier in life, if you're in a constant state of terror; your brain is shaped to be on alert for danger, and to try to make those terrible feelings go away." But positive experiences, he asserts, can retrain the brain. We need "experiences that deeply and viscerally contradict the helplessness, rage or collapse that result from trauma." Some of us have suffered horribly, but consistent, loving, supportive, patient engagement can slowly change the "wiring" in our brains.[24]

A well-known author and speaker came to our church, and I had dinner with him. During our conversation, he told me that in his entire life he had never heard his father say, "I love you," and it broke his heart. This makes me even more thankful for the amazing atmosphere of love that my mom and dad provided for my brother and me. I remember a PSA from years ago that asked, "Have you hugged your kid today?" I could always say, "Yes, they hugged me! And they told me they loved me! Multiple times every day, in fact!" There was never a doubt that they loved me. But I also realize that a lot of people have some pretty significant deficits in their brain wiring as a result of not feeling safe and loved, so it's harder for them to reject lies and believe the truths of the gospel. I'm not giving them a pass, and actually, they don't want a pass. They just want people to understand them, have some patience with them, and help them experience the warmth, safety, and honesty today that they missed when they were young. God has made us amazingly resilient, and people can be healed from childhood trauma which produced their ingrained fear and shame. Sometimes the healing is sudden and miraculous, but far more often, it's the product of a long season of experiencing the love of God imparted through people who care for them.

Every day when I wake up, I think about God's love for me. I imagine Him looking at me and smiling the way I used to stand over Connor and Logan's beds when they were little boys and smiled at them. I was so glad they're my sons, and I was sure God loved me even more than that! But that's not the experience of many people.

When I was a young pastor, sometimes people in our church would give a prophetic word to someone, "The Lord says He loves you." It happened often enough that I was, well, a little annoyed. I thought, *Okay, we know that. Can't we move on to things we don't know?* But now, as I've met with so many people who struggle to grasp the tender, affectionate love of God, my perspective has flipflopped. When anyone gives this word, I want to shout, "Bring it on! Say it again! We can't get too much of that!" I'm convinced that a lot of people who sit in church each week believe that God is royally displeased with them, and at best, He tolerates them. That idea was unfathomable to me years ago, but now I realize this faulty concept of God is far more common than I used to think.

Just in case you need to hear it, let me say it again: God loves you so much that He sent His Son Jesus into this world to die to pay the penalty for your sins and forgive you. Now, that's love! Embrace His love. Embrace Him.

A BETTER VOICE

Matthew takes us to the remarkable scene when Jesus went down to the Jordan River to be baptized by His cousin John: "After his baptism, as Jesus came up out of the water, the heavens were opened and he saw the Spirit of God descending like a dove and settling on him. And a voice from heaven said, 'This is my dearly loved Son, who brings me great joy'" (Matthew 3:16-17). Here we have the Trinity represented: the Son being baptized for His mission, the empowering Spirit descending on Him, and the affirming voice of the Father. I can imagine that the voice of the Father was stuck in Jesus' mind and heart for the rest of His days, but then, He had enjoyed unbroken and unlimited love from eternity past.

One of the recurring concepts in the Scriptures is that we are "in Christ," or "in Him," or "in the Beloved." That means that God sees us as His beloved, too. Later in Jesus' life, on the night He was arrested, He prayed to the Father. In the long, beautiful prayer John recorded, Jesus poured out His heart: "I have given them the glory you gave me, so they may be one as we are one. I am in them and you are in me. May they experience such perfect unity that the world will know that you sent me and that you love them as much as you love me. Father, I want these whom you have given me to be with me where I am. Then they can see all the glory you gave me because you loved me even before the world began!" (John 17:22-24)

Let Him heal your broken places, and be thrilled that He delights in you.

Did you catch that? ". . . that you love them as much as you love me." It's astounding! Right now, at this moment, the Father loves you as much as He loves Jesus, and that will never change. Let that sink deep into your soul, and let it find and fill the crevices of doubt, fear, hurt, and shame you've tried to keep hidden.

Let Him heal your broken places, and be thrilled that He delights in you.

Many people are equipped for mental siege warfare by memorizing some biblical affirmations. Here are a few to chew on:

> I'm a child of God. (Romans 8:16)

> I'm totally forgiven. (Ephesians 4:31—5:2)

> I'm saved by God's great grace. (Ephesians 2:8-9)

> I'm a partaker in the divine nature. (2 Peter 1:4)

> I'm the temple of the Holy Spirit. (1 Corinthians 6:19-20)

> I'm an overcomer. (John 16:33; Revelation 2:7)

> I'm a new creature in Christ. (2 Corinthians 5:17)

> I'm the light of the world and the salt of the earth. (Matthew 5:13-14)

> And one that's not an "I am" but is one of my favorites: The Father loves me as much as He loves Jesus. (John 17:23)

Sometimes (for some of us, quite often), we need to have a heart-to-heart talk with ourselves. This isn't some kind of personality disorder or strange incantation; it's thoroughly biblical, and we find it many times in the Psalms. These poems communicate the full range of human experience, from the highest delights and praise to God to the deepest depths of despair and resentment. In

Psalm 42, the writer is really bummed, and he pours out his heart to God. He begins,

> As the deer pants for streams of water,
>   so my soul pants for you, my God.
> My soul thirsts for God, for the living God.
>   When can I go and meet with God?
> My tears have been my food
>   day and night,
> while people say to me all day long,
>   "Where is your God?"

Then he takes himself by the shirt collar (or robe collar in that day), and gives himself a pep talk:

> Why, my soul, are you downcast?
>   Why so disturbed within me?
> Put your hope in God,
>   for I will yet praise him,
>   my Savior and my God.

But he's not through. He cascades into another round of heartache, wondering why God seems to have abandoned him. But again, he doesn't settle for prolonged self-pity. He looks in the mirror and repeats what his soul needs to hear:

> Why, my soul, are you downcast?
>   Why so disturbed within me?

Put your hope in God,
    for I will yet praise him,
        my Savior and my God. (Psalm 42:1-3, 5, 11 NIV)

For years I've used a particular wordplay to reinforce my biblical identity. Quite often, when we meet someone, we ask them and they ask us, "What do you do for a living?" That's not a terrible question, but perhaps a better direction is to say, "Tell me about yourself." This focuses more on identity than performance. I've learned to apply this concept far more broadly. For instance, I no longer say, "I do exercises." Instead, I say, "I'm healthy." I no longer say, "I'm giving to the mission of the church." I say, "I'm generous." The seemingly minor difference takes the focus away from my performance and onto my identity. That matters to me. When my "I am's" are clear and strong, my "I do's" soon fall in line.

Words themselves don't have power, but the person behind them has incredible power . . . for good or for harm. Memorizing biblical truth statements is important, and we need to remember that God's heart is woven in and through all of them. He is the one who loves, He is the one who provides, He is the one who brings light out of darkness, He is the one who mends the broken places, and He is the one who gives our lives meaning and hope.

LIVING ABOVE THE CLOUDS

I remember flying back to Minneapolis on a spring day. Clouds blanketed the city and the surrounding area, but above the clouds, the sun was shining brightly. We flew through the dense cloudbank to land, and as we taxied to the gate, the scene was very different: gloomy and drizzly. A lot of us live below the clouds. We feel the despair, the stress of work and family, the anger in our culture, and the loss of people we love. The gloom feels like more than emotions—it feels like a heavy, wet blanket thrown over us. Is it possible to experience joy and gratitude in the middle of the struggles we face each day? Yes, but only if we learn to live above the clouds where the sun still shines.

Paul knew something about struggles because he had more than his fair share. In his last letter to the Corinthians, he needed them to see that he had sacrificed and suffered for Jesus, for the gospel, and for those who were hearing the letter read to them. His brief list of hardships helps us understand his tenacious commitment to God's grace and the people who needed to experience it. He wrote:

I have worked harder, been put in prison more often, been whipped times without number, and faced death again and again. Five different times the Jewish leaders gave me thirty-nine lashes. Three times I was beaten with rods. Once I was stoned. Three times I was shipwrecked. Once I spent a whole night and a day adrift at sea. I have traveled on many long journeys. I have faced danger from rivers and from robbers. I have faced danger from my own people, the Jews, as well as from the Gentiles. I have faced danger in the cities, in the deserts, and on the seas. And I have faced danger from men who claim to be believers but are not. I have worked hard and long, enduring many sleepless nights. I have been hungry and thirsty and have often gone without food. I have shivered in the cold, without enough clothing to keep me warm.

Then, besides all this, I have the daily burden of my concern for all the churches. Who is weak without my feeling that weakness? Who is led astray, and I do not burn with anger? (2 Corinthians 11:23-29)

What kept Paul going? What lifted him above the clouds? Faith, hope, and love. In one of the most beautiful and powerful passages in the New Testament, Paul reassures us that God's love never fails . . . never, never, never. He wrote to the believers in Rome:

Can anything ever separate us from Christ's love? Does it mean he no longer loves us if we have trouble or calamity, or are persecuted, or hungry, or destitute, or in danger, or threatened with death? (As the Scriptures say, "For your sake we are killed every day; we are being slaughtered like sheep.") No, despite all these things, overwhelming victory is ours through Christ, who loved us.

And I am convinced that nothing can ever separate us from God's love. Neither death nor life, neither angels nor demons, neither our fears for today nor our worries about tomorrow—not even the powers of hell can separate us from God's love. No power in the sky above or in the earth below—indeed, nothing in all creation will ever be able to separate us from the love of God that is revealed in Christ Jesus our Lord. (Romans 8:35-39)

What has the power to force us to live beneath the clouds? Trouble, ridicule, or hunger? No. Death? Not at all. Demons? Nope. Fears and worries? No way. The power of hell, the powers of creation, and the powers of the dark forces? No, nothing. We are more than conquerors! Not by our wisdom, strength, and wit, but by God's love and power. In *Walking with God through Pain and Suffering,* pastor and author Tim Keller encourages us, "Suffering can refine us rather than destroy us because God himself walks with us in the fire."[25]

We may or may not be able to escape our troubles, but if we must endure them, we can have *faith* that God is with us, *hope* that His purpose will be fulfilled, and an experience of His *love* every step of the way.

CONSIDER THIS:

1. What's the lesson behind the story of the eagle and the chicken?

2. The ten fearful spies saw the same things Caleb and Joshua saw. What do you think was the difference in their responses? Who in the story do you relate to? Explain your answer.

3. Can you identify with my "death spiral" of self-condemning thoughts? If you can, when does this happen to you? How would it help to anticipate it before it happens?

4. How would you describe the voices you heard and internalized as you were growing up? How do you think they have affected you?

5. What are two or three of the most powerful affirmations in the list in this chapter (or others you've seen before)? What impact do they have on your self-concept?

6. Look at the selected verses from Psalm 42. How would it (or does it) affect you to speak to yourself like this?

7. What steps will you take to "live above the clouds"?

CHAPTER 8

◢ BENCHMARKS

People often say that motivation doesn't last. Well, neither does bathing—that's why we recommend it daily.

—Zig Ziglar

After that embarrassing conversation with Becca years ago about my weight, I set a goal to lose thirty pounds. From what I could tell, all the excess fat was in my gut and my face. I assume that I had gained the excess weight over a long period of time . . . which is another way of saying that I made excuses over and over again. Today, when I look at the before and after pictures, I can't believe that I let my weight gain go so long.

Actually, I soon realized that my goal wasn't sustainable, and I gained back about four pounds. That's the sweet spot for me. But just as gradually, I began to rationalize eating a larger helping, a whole dessert, or an unhealthy snack, and I noticed that my medium shirt felt a bit tight. It was fine when I stood up, but when I was sitting, the pull on the buttons caused my shirt to separate. I went from "medium right" to "medium tight." I still had some shirts I'd worn before losing weight. They were in the "large loose" category. When I pulled one of them off the rack in my closet and held it up, it looked like a colorful sail for an America's Cup yacht.

That was my wakeup call, my benchmark, my red flag. It was time to go back on my diet so I could get down to "medium right" again. I had to identify the excuses I'd used over the previous weeks and months that got me off track. If I couldn't identify them, I didn't stand much of a chance of defeating them the next time . . . and next time was always just around the corner! It wasn't that hard to know what went wrong: I'd stopped walking regularly, I'd been on the road and made some bad decisions about my food choices, I had whole desserts twice in a row because they were so good, and I ate whatever snack was offered instead of sticking with almonds or something else healthy to eat.

Maybe I was raised to get my money's worth from "all you can eat" buffets, or maybe I never wanted to offend a cook by not eating everything that was put in front of me. Whatever the reason, the pattern of overeating is obviously counterproductive. When I eat too much, I'm sluggish and lethargic. I'm not as sharp mentally, and I find myself drifting when I'm talking to people. But when I work out and eat well, I'm more energetic, more creative, and more attentive.

Long-distance runners get a kick of endorphins, called a "runner's high," when you'd think they'd be utterly exhausted. When I'm on top of my game, I get a "pastor's high" and can keep going when others are fading. The payoffs are abundantly clear: there are negative consequences of making bad choices, and there are big benefits for doing what I need to do to stay healthy and strong. I'm radically, totally committed to making good choices about my health. Becca is my CAP: chief accountability partner. Together, we make sure I work out every day. I feel *so* much better when I do!

When I attended an airshow of experimental aircraft, I heard one of the pilots talk about flying in bad weather. His repeated refrain was, "Trust your instruments. It may feel like you're in a dive, but watch your altimeter. If it's level, you're flying straight and true. When your mind tells you that you're in a steep dive, everything in you may want to panic, but trust your instruments.

They're not lying. They're not broken." What are our instruments? The bathroom scale, the voice of affirmation or criticism from a spouse, feedback at work, our level of energy and enthusiasm, and things like that . . . things that are as evident as an altimeter on the instrument panel in front of a pilot.

If we pay attention, we don't have to wait for a crash to identify retrograde benchmarks.

If we pay attention, we don't have to wait for a crash to identify retrograde benchmarks. If we're using excuses, the red light is already flashing! And we're pretty creative in avoiding responsibility. For instance, a guy might tell himself he just wants to read an article about the NBA, but surprise, it's found in the *Sports Illustrated* swimsuit issue! Or he spends hours fantasizing about winning the lottery and imagining all the stuff he can buy . . . and the envy he'll elicit from his friends. Or she angles for a promotion at work to prove to herself and anyone watching that the boss considers her competent and valuable. Now, there's nothing inherently wrong with sex, beauty, money, and accomplishment, unless they shove Jesus out of His rightful place in the center of our lives. If they're gifts from God, we can enjoy them within the boundaries He created and without guilt, fear, or shame. But if they become our primary pursuits, they inevitably result in, you guessed it, guilt, fear, and shame.

If comparison is a problem for men, it's a plague for women. I'm a people-watcher, and I've noticed that in any public place— the mall, the ballpark, church, or any other gathering—women check out other women more than men check them out. They're looking at everything: clothes, hair, makeup, shape, complexion, purse, jewelry, shoes . . . each part of the package. Comparison produces the twin poisons of jealousy and envy: jealousy is worrying that someone will take what you have; envy is wanting what the other person has. Both are powered by a deep sense of discontent—"I'm getting a raw deal! I deserve better . . . and more!" Some people wilt into self-pity, but others redouble their efforts—and their spending—to keep up.

Gen Z, the youngest adults among us, suffer from what my son Logan calls "the thirst trap." They're thirsty for attention, so they make themselves vulnerable online, hoping people will come to their rescue and tell them how wonderful they are. It's this generation's version of fishing for compliments, but it's powered by social media, which makes people far more vulnerable . . . and far more needy when they either get or don't get the attention they crave. The people responding with encouragement see that it's possible to get what they, too, crave, so the cycle of need and rescue exponentially repeats and multiplies. Of course, temptations aren't limited by gender, age, or status. We're equal opportunity desperate cravers!

THE STRUGGLE MAKES US STRONGER

One of the most important benchmarks of progress (or slippage) is our response to life's challenges, but who in his right mind would gladly invite heartache and trials into his life? This kind of courageous response only makes sense if we believe there's a payoff somewhere down the line. For instance, people are more than willing to sacrifice comfort for a higher purpose. They spend time studying and learning a vocation so they can have a meaningful career. They exercise, seemingly feeling weaker from the exertion, but actually grow stronger. They take time and energy to love people who can't repay them, to give to causes that have eternal value, and serve people who may never know their names.

But heartaches and trials? That's often a different story. We don't want any of that! And we're shocked—shocked!—when we face setbacks and losses. We must have used a black highlighter in our Bibles in places where God promises we'll endure suffering, like what Jesus told His disciples (and us) on the night He was betrayed. He wanted them to understand what was going to happen over the next twenty-four hours as He was arrested, tried, tortured, and killed. He warned them, "But the time is coming—indeed it's here now—when you will be scattered, each one going his own way, leaving me alone. Yet I am not alone because the Father is with me. I have told you all this so that you may have peace in me. Here on earth you will have many trials and sorrows. But take heart, because I have overcome the world" (John 16:32-33). Jesus didn't say that "you *may* have many trials and sorrows," or "there's a chance you *could* experience trials and sorrows." The fact is that trials and sorrows are a normal part of life, especially for those who have answered the call to follow the "Suffering Servant" who gave himself for others.

At the end of his life, as Paul looked back on the thirty years or so of suffering to extend the kingdom of God throughout the known world, he could reflect:

> As for me, my life has already been poured out as an offering to God. The time of my death is near. I have fought the good fight, I have finished the race, and I have remained faithful. And now the prize awaits me—the crown of

righteousness, which the Lord, the righteous Judge, will give me on the day of his return. And the prize is not just for me but for all who eagerly look forward to his appearing. (2 Timothy 4:6-8)

Man, I want that to be my testimony, too! But the way to get there isn't to wish for affluence and the absence of struggle. It's to wade into difficulties and trust God to do what only He can do: turn them into stepping-stones for us and turn us into examples for others to follow.

The fight is very real for all of us, and in our relatively comfortable culture, maybe the biggest fight is against misplaced expectations that God has promised a life of ease and plenty. Paul reminded the Ephesians, "Be strong in the Lord and in his mighty power. Put on all of God's armor so that you will be able to stand firm against all strategies of the devil. For we are not fighting against flesh-and-blood enemies, but against evil rulers and authorities of the unseen world, against mighty powers in this dark world, and against evil spirits in the heavenly places" (Ephesians 6:10-12).

Charles Spurgeon was one of the most gifted and powerful preachers the church has ever known. He led a huge and popular church in London in the latter part of the nineteenth century. As a leader, he felt the pressure to stay strong in the middle of opposition and discouragement, and he was well aware that the enemy was both powerful and crafty. He pulled the curtain back for us:

And do you think the devil is pleased with you? I tell you no. If you had seen Satan the moment you were converted, you would have beheld a wondrous scene. As soon as you gave your heart to Christ, Satan spread his bat-like-wings—down he flew into Hell—and summoning all his counselors he said, "Sons of the pit, true heirs of darkness, you who once were clad in light but who fell with me from high dignities—another of my servants has forsaken me. I have lost another of my family. He is gone over to the side of the Lord of Hosts. Oh you, my compeers, you fellow helpers of the powers of darkness, leave no stone unturned to destroy him. I bid you all hurl all your fiercest darts at him. Plague him. Let Hell dogs bark at him. Let fiends besiege him. Give him no rest, harass him to the death. Let the fumes of our corrupt and burning lake ever rise in his nostrils. Persecute him, the man is a traitor, give him no peace! Since I cannot have him here to bind him in chains of adamant. Since I never can have him here to torment and afflict him, as long as you can, till his dying day, I bid you howl at him! Until he crosses the river, afflict him, grieve him, torment him. For the wretch has turned against me and become a servant of the Lord." Such may have been the scene in Hell that very day when you did love the Lord. And do you think Satan loves you better, now? Ah, no. He will always be at you, for your enemy, "like a roaring lion, goes about seeking whom he may devour."[26]

In the opening lines of Paul's last letter to the Corinthians, he gives us a glimpse into his emotional life. At one point, he felt so beaten down and discouraged that he wasn't sure he would live. He explained, "We do not want you to be uninformed, brothers and sisters, about the troubles we experienced in the province of Asia. We were under great pressure, far beyond our ability to endure, so that we despaired of life itself. Indeed, we felt we had received the sentence of death. But this happened that we might not rely on ourselves but on God, who raises the dead" (2 Corinthians 1:8-9 NIV).

There's a big difference between *a death sentence* and *a sentence of death.* A death sentence is punishment for a capital offense; a sentence of death happens when we do the right things but the enemy tries to kill us. It's a very dark place, one that Jesus experienced in Gethsemane and Paul suffered in his ministry. The hope of Jesus and Paul was in this life *and* in the one to come. In other words, whatever happens, God is present, faithful, and trustworthy. Let me draw a few conclusions from Paul's experience:

> Suffering opens our hearts to be consoled by God. A few verses earlier, Paul explained that when he was at his lowest point, God met him there: "Praise be to the God and Father of our Lord Jesus Christ, the Father of compassion and the God of all comfort, who comforts us in all our troubles, so that we can comfort those in any trouble with the comfort we ourselves receive from God. For just as we share abundantly in the sufferings of Christ, so also our comfort abounds through Christ" (vv. 3-5). As we've seen, heartaches surface our vulnerability. When this happens, some of us close our hearts to protect us from getting hurt any more, but others open our hearts to the compassion, kindness, and strength Jesus provides.

> Our best friendships are forged during times of distress. Throughout this passage, Paul uses the plural: *we* and *our.* He

continues, "He has delivered us from such a deadly peril, and he will deliver us again. On him we have set our hope that he will continue to deliver us, as you help us by your prayers. Then many will give thanks on our behalf for the gracious favor granted us in answer to the prayers of many" (vv. 10-11). That's true for all of us. When you think about the people who know you best and love you the most, the ones you trust, the ones you call at 2 o'clock in the morning when you need a friend, those relationships didn't just happen. They are the product of being there for each other, caring when others have walked away, and praying when others have given up hope.

> In our time of desperate need, we find God to be present and faithful. I've heard many people say that during a time of crisis and concern, they felt closer to God than ever before. Most of them would say they wouldn't trade that closeness for good health, financial stability, or anything else they used to value so highly. Our extremity is God's opportunity—first to open our hearts to himself in fresh, powerful ways, and then to open doors to new possibilities. Isaiah assures us:

> But now, this is what the Lord says—
>> he who created you, Jacob,
>> he who formed you, Israel:
> "Do not fear, for I have redeemed you;
>> I have summoned you by name; you are mine.
> When you pass through the waters,
>> I will be with you;
> and when you pass through the rivers,
>> they will not sweep over you.

When you walk through the fire,
>   you will not be burned;
>   the flames will not set you ablaze.
For I am the Lord your God,
>   the Holy One of Israel, your Savior . . ."
(Isaiah 43:1-3)

When Jesus prayed in Gethsemane and asked the Father to let the cup of judgment pass from Him, He was alone. His closest friends were asleep. And when Jesus was dying on the cross, His Father turned His back so He could make the full payment for our sins. Jesus suffered loneliness in our place so that we can be sure we're never alone. He's with us in our Gethsemane, and He's with us as we follow Him and carry our crosses.

> Suffering also strips away complacency and surfaces the power of God. When Paul faced the sentence of death for his faithfulness, one of the results was that "we might not rely on ourselves but on God, who raises the dead." What was he saying? When we come to the end of ourselves, we begin to experience the glory of God. When we're at our weakest, we realize the awesome power of God. When we're empty, God fills us with His presence and purpose. This is, to say the least, the opposite of how the world operates. All around us, people value personal power, domination, fame, wealth, and applause . . . it's all about them! But we're citizens of the upside-down kingdom where admitting we're powerless gives us power, admitting we're sinners reveals the depths of God's forgiveness, and confessing we're unworthy opens the door

to the thrill of knowing we've been adopted by the God of the universe.

> Seeing God's faithfulness in difficulties gives us stories worth telling. What kind of stories do you love to hear? Bland narratives of passivity? No way! We love dramas, with terrible trouble, cliffhanger moments, and glorious rescues. Our struggles can become the backstory of the best stories of our lives, times when we see God occasionally work miracles, but more often, how He gives us courage to keep taking one step after another until His glory is revealed. The couple who came very close to losing their marriage now gives hope to those who are wondering if they can go on. The person who had weight problems for years but has made remarkable progress is a source of encouragement for those who aren't sure anything will work for them. The examples are endless—if we're walking with God, we've had to overcome something, so we have a story to tell. It's okay to have cheerleaders who tell us everything will be okay, but what we really need is a coach, a guide, a fellow traveler who has already been on the road and can show us the way.

> A faithful response to a struggle prepares us to say "yes" to the next one. We may wish we could orchestrate our lives to eliminate every pain and every difficulty, but that's not going to happen in this life. We're creatures of habit: if our habit is to run from difficulties, we'll establish a lifestyle of complaining and blaming, but if we build a new habit of trusting God in the middle of the storm, we won't be shocked or thrown off balance when we encounter the next one. And be sure of this: it's coming.

If you'll look to God instead of trusting in your talent, wisdom, and grit, and if you'll humble yourself to realize that God uses pain to teach life's greatest lessons, the struggle will make you stronger.

> If you'll look to God instead of trusting in your talent, wisdom, and grit, and if you'll humble yourself to realize that God uses pain to teach life's greatest lessons, the struggle will make you stronger. It's ironic, but people who have critical change issues (like alcoholics, addicts, people with eating disorders, etc.) often have a better grasp of this principle than the rest of us who deal with chronic problems. They've come to the end of themselves, and they realize there's no hope in trying to paper over their struggles any longer. If they've been in recovery long enough, they've begun to see new sources of strength, beauty, friendship, and truth they've never known before.

In a sermon during Covid, I told people that if they were overweight, they needed to be extra careful because the statistics showed that overweight people often got sicker than others. I wasn't prepared for the blowback. I thought my struggles with weight gave me permission to address this problem in other people . . . but boy, was I wrong! Several of our pastors observed that some of those who were most upset weren't overweight, but they were taking up the cause for people who were. They were vicariously offended . . . which is part of the social media outrage machine. Let me ask: are there people in your life who are defending your bad habits to be your hero, but their defense is actually preventing you from making progress? We need people who love us enough to be brutally honest with us and help us take steps forward.

REMINDERS

It's helpful to have statements that warn us that we may be getting off track, as well as voices that remind us to stay on track. For instance, my weight mantra is "large loose, medium tight, medium right." My shirt sizes are excellent benchmarks for me. In the recovery world, people watch out for triggers that make them vulnerable to want to drink or use, and they use an acronym as a warning: HALT stands for hungry, angry, lonely, and tired. Another warning benchmark is starting a sentence with, "I might as well . . ." This happens when people have slipped a little, but instead of coming back, they're discouraged and continue down the slippery slope of excuses and poor choices. We can become our own worst enemies. It's called "self-sabotage," and it happens when a choice or a habit undermines our goals and creates guilt, fear, and isolation. Addictions of all kinds are a form of self-harm, but we also exercise self-destructive behavior when we tell ourselves we're hopeless, worthless, and helpless. Some of us call ourselves horrible names, but almost always under our breath or in our minds. A guy told me about the names he called himself, and I asked, "What would you say if someone called somebody else those names?" He thought for a few seconds and then said, "I'd say he hated him." He got the point: he hated himself. It came from years of his dad telling him he was a failure, and he had internalized those messages. From that moment, he realized the source of those thoughts, and he began to recognize them quickly so he could replace them with life-affirming biblical truths.

As benchmarks to remind us to make good food choices, when Becca and I are tempted, we tell each other: "You can't out-run the fork." And, "It's not worth the treadmill." In 1984, Dunkin Donuts had a commercial showing an exhausted baker leaving his house very early in the morning with a look of resignation on his face and moaning, "It's time to make the donuts." Becca and I have adapted it; when we really don't want to exercise, we tell each other, "It's time to make the donuts . . . disappear." It's a silly statement, but it immediately prompts motivation, decision, and action to get dressed and get going.

We have other statements to remind us about good habits: "Stay close to the joy" and "Blessed to be a blessing."

Here are a few you might want to use . . .

> "Fill your life with experiences, not things. Have stories to tell, not stuff to show."

> "Before talking, please connect the tongue to the brain."

> "If a cookie falls on the floor, and you pick it up, that's a squat, right?"

> "I'm in charge of my life's story."

> "The past has no power over me anymore."

> "I can. I will."

> "I'm not my mistakes."

> "I don't judge my past because I don't live there anymore."

> "Life offers a second chance. It's called tomorrow."

> "If you can smell yourself, others have been able to for a while."

> And my favorite: "If at first you don't succeed, don't try skydiving!"

The evening news in Austin, Texas, showed four people in a boat on Lady Bird Lake near downtown. Nothing special there, but a third of the boat was hanging over the edge of the thirty-six-foot-high Longhorn Dam. When the Police Department was notified, they launched a patrol boat, sped to the scene, and threw a rope to tie to the boat. They backed it off the dam, and no one was hurt.

Officer Smith explained to news teams that two buoys mark the danger zone at the dam, but the boaters either didn't see them or ignored them. By the time the boat passed the buoys, the force of the water going over the dam pulled the boat toward the edge. District Commander Joshua Todd told reporters, "You got to remember that water is a pretty powerful force in nature. And even on a clear, calm day in an urban area, things can go wrong very, very quickly."

What's the point of this story? It's a metaphor of an experience we want to avoid! We can miss the warning signs. Everything looks fine, but failure to take precautions can have dangerous and deadly consequences. In our experience, the tug toward the edge of the dam may be spending too much money, not spending enough time at home, the scourge of comparison, self-sabotage in countless ways, or dabbling again with addictions and compulsions. Whatever it may be, all of us are in the boat, and the dam isn't far away. As the Austin police officers would tell us, the lessons are very clear: first, look for the warning buoys, and second, stay out of the powerful current pulling us into danger.

Stay alert to the benchmarks. Don't go over the dam.

Don't worry about the world coming to an end today. It's already tomorrow in Australia.

—*Charles Schulz*

CONSIDER THIS:

1. As you read my story of weight gain and my three benchmarks of shirts ("medium right," "medium tight," and "large loose"), did any benchmarks come to mind for you? If so, what are they, and how did you initially respond when you first noticed them?

2. What are some ways the culture's promises of ease, plenty, and fun make us think we shouldn't ever have to suffer? How do these promises affect us?

3. People say that suffering makes us "bitter or better." How have you seen both of these outcomes in the lives of people you know?

4. Look again at Isaiah 43:1-3. Do you really believe that your "extremity is God's opportunity"? Explain your answer.

5. Whose stories of faith and hope in the midst of suffering do you admire? What gave that person (or those people) the courage to face trials with such strength?

6. What are the specific buoys you need to notice (and keep noticing)? What will paying attention to them do for you? What are some consequences of ignoring them?

CHAPTER 9

◢ THE GAME WITHIN THE GAME

The game within the game is the game that only the players see. They experience it in relation to one another on the floor at a particular time and in the middle of the action. It is one of the nuances of the game of basketball.

—*Walt Frazier, NBA star*

In every sport, there's the contest the fans see, but each player knows there's a more personal, more specific, more intense game within the game. We look at the offense come to the line in a football game, and the defense spreads out, but the real contest is between the right tackle and the defensive end, between the wide receiver and the cornerback, between the offensive coordinator who calls the plays and the defensive coordinator who positions his guys to stop them. Even in individual sports like tennis, the real game is more than forehands and backhands; it's the inner strength to try a risky shot at a pivotal point in the game, or the mental lapse that can come from being too upset too long at a bad call.

In the 1997 NBA Finals, the Chicago Bulls played the Utah Jazz. As always, it was a best of seven series. The Jazz had some of the best players in the history of the league in Karl Malone and John Stockton. The Bulls had a number of stars, but none shined brighter than Michael Jordan. Commentators were divided in their predictions, and true to form, the team split the first four games. The team that won Game 5 in Salt Lake City would have a big advantage. At 2:00 in the morning of gameday, Jordan called his trainer to come to his hotel room. When he arrived, the star was in a fetal position on the floor, sweating and in pain. The trainer helped him crawl back into bed. At the time, people assumed he had the flu, but it was probably food poisoning from pizza a few hours before. The Bulls' trainers were sure Jordan would miss the game that was scheduled to start at 7:00 that night.

The Jazz hadn't lost a home game during the postseason, and a win would give them an edge when they went back to Chicago. All day, the Bulls created strategies to maximize the rest of the players' talents, but just before 6:00, Jordan got out of bed, went to the Delta Center, and dressed for the game. His temperature was 103. The commentators and fans were shocked that he was on the floor, and it was obvious he wasn't himself. The Jazz rolled to a 36-20 lead in the second quarter, but somehow, Jordan started making shots, scoring 17 points in the quarter. When Coach Phil Jackson put Jordan on the bench to rest, the Jazz took advantage, building an 8-point lead. With Jordan back in and scoring 15 in the fourth, the Bulls found themselves down by a point with less than a minute remaining. Jordan was fouled, made the first free throw but missed the second. The Bulls got the rebound and passed to an open Jordan, who nailed a 3-point shot. The final seconds were frantic, but the Bulls held on to win by 2. With seconds remaining and the game in hand, Jordan collapsed into a teammates arms, immortalizing what was already called "The Flu Game."

In basketball, every matchup is a game within the game, but in this particular contest, Jordan not only played one-on-one against his defender; he also played against his ailing body. He finished with 38 points, five assists, three steals, and a block. The Bulls won the next game in Chicago to take the series four games to two, but the only game people remember is the time Michael Jordan stepped onto the court with a high fever and willed his way to a win.

Years ago at a conference, I heard Joe Gibbs, the former head coach of the Washington Redskins, explain how he manufactured an additional incentive for his defensive linemen and linebackers. The Walkman had just come on the market, and it was the newest, coolest gadget around. Before a game, Gibbs held one up and said, "If one of you gets a quarterback sack today, this baby is yours!" One of the burly defensive linemen growled, "I'm gonna get two of them!" He could have gone to the store and bought hundreds of them, but that wasn't the point. Coach Gibbs crafted a game within the game so his players would be more motivated than ever to play well. Sure enough, the lineman got two sacks that day, and he got his prize of two Walkmans. The next week, Gibbs upped the ante. He told the players, "Whoever gets a sack today gets a leather recliner." Boom! These guys played their hearts out . . . for a chair they could easily have bought on their own.

FRESH, NEW GOALS

When I approached my 50th birthday, I created a game within the game of my health. I had lost significant weight a few years before, but I determined that by this birthday I would be in the best shape of my life. For the weddings of our sons Connor and Logan, Becca determined to get in her best shape ever. No one but me knew she was playing a game within a game. (She's not the only mother-of-the-groom to do this!)

This strategy creates goals and stirs motivation to compete with yourself to accomplish something significant. Would you have done it anyway? Maybe, but maybe not. Identifying a new incentive is important to propel us forward, especially when we're already making pretty good progress and we're tempted to become a bit lethargic.

Identifying a new incentive is important to propel us forward, especially when we're already making pretty good progress and we're tempted to become a bit lethargic.

This is beyond "I still . . ." This is a higher goal, a deeper drive, a bigger win. Instead of paying down debt to a more manageable level, consider a higher mark of paying it all off, paying off your mortgage, and having a certain amount in savings and investments by a particular date. Instead of just having a date night every week, go on a mini-vacation with your spouse every quarter, and go to a place you both love. Instead of just having a goal of keeping your kids alive until they graduate from high school, invest in their future with classes that tap into their interests. Instead of coasting, find new interests and develop new skills. If you've been satisfied with your eighteen handicap in golf, press yourself to get it down to twelve. I've made it my goal to watch fifty-two TED talks and read fifty-two books every year. This isn't just busy work; it keeps me fresh, stimulates my mind, and gives me interesting things to talk about with my family, friends, and staff team.

Some of us have been so far in the hole that getting back to zero is a major accomplishment. I get that, it's real progress, but it's not the abundant life! If your life is a train wreck, trust God and work hard to get back to even, but when you get there, don't stop. Look for opportunities to grow . . . and create your own opportunities.

When people face change, many of them moan, "Oh, no," but I'm different. I want to shout, "Oh, man!" I see change as a chance to try something new, go places I've never been, and see success I've never experienced. Yes, I know. A lot of people feel uncomfortable with change. Wisdom is the ability to sort out rational concern from crippling fear. Believe me: I'm not advocating insanity! People may resist change because old habits feel safe, they already feel overwhelmed with current stresses, they've never seen the proposed change work out, or they can only see the potential problems in the new idea.[27] As a pastor, husband, and father, my job is to show people the benefits of change. When they're persuaded that the good might surpass the threat of loss or pain, they'll be open to the process of change. I find that when people aren't given enough information, they fill the empty spaces with doubts and fears. Knowledge, then, is power.

I see every potential change, every challenge, and every open door as a new tool in my toolbox. When a craftsman gets a new tool, he learns how to use it, and if it proves to make him more skilled, he keeps it around to use whenever it's needed. To use a very different metaphor, in video games, meeting a challenge propels the player to the next level where a new challenge awaits. The thrill of the game is moving higher, tackling harder tasks, and then moving on again. You have to do the quest to beat the boss to get the piece of armor that makes it easier to move up. I don't shy away from difficulties or higher goals because I know that if I rise to the occasion, I'll be more prepared for the next one. Over the years, I've learned that I may need additional resources to meet a challenge: a new skill, a new coach, a new mentor, or a new strategy. I'm not at all surprised that I need help. That's just part of the deal.

A little creativity goes a long way. Early in our church's history, I realized the most boring time in the worship service was the announcements. We tried to shorten them, be more enthusiastic about them, and craft them to have more punch, but nothing worked. We knew we had to give our people information, so the staff designed a game within the game: one Sunday, we told the person making the announcements that he had to find a way to say the word "Birkenstocks" at some point. I've never looked forward to announcements more in my life! He pulled it off beautifully: "Today we're having our church picnic. You can come in your running shoes, your sandals, or your Birkenstocks." When Connor was in choir, they performed the same songs every day—for weeks. He and some other students found ways to rephrase a line or wave to someone in the audience to spice things up and entertain themselves . . . without incurring the wrath of the choir director.

"A rut is just a grave with both ends knocked out."

Routine is important, but only to a point. After that, it becomes a rut, and you know what they say, "A rut is just a grave with both ends knocked out." Find things that push you to try something new. It can be profound, or it can be silly, but try things. I know someone who occasionally brushes his teeth with his off hand. It feels awkward and odd, but it strengthens your brain. . . and it's free!

In my yearly goals, I work on a virtue to be more like Jesus, and this makes me more aware of these virtues when I see them in others. For instance, not long ago, I was with a friend running an errand to repair a golf club. As he handed the club to the guy behind the counter, my friend stopped and asked him, "How are you doing today? Things going okay for you?" The man looked up and made eye contact. It was obvious that my friend was one of very few people who saw him as a living, breathing human being instead of just a dehumanized fixer. I thought, *Huh . . . that made a difference in that guy's life.* A few minutes later as we left the store, a family was on their way in, and my friend took a few extra seconds to hold the door for them. As we walked away, I told him, "I noticed how you treated the guy at the desk, and then how you stopped to open the door for that family. What's that about?"

He shrugged like he was a bit embarrassed, and then he told me, "Yeah, I've been thinking about the need to show kindness more often to more people. So this year, I'm being more intentional. As I follow Jesus, I want to represent more of His heart of kindness and compassion."

A little thoughtfulness, a simple gesture, a big impact.

FOLLOW THE PROMPTS

Most of us at least occasionally feel an internal nudge, sometimes to do something and sometimes to avoid doing something. Perhaps shaped in our backgrounds, perhaps in our DNA, our conscience is an inner voice to show us right from wrong, wisdom from foolishness, moving ahead from being passive. Christians have that and more; we have the Holy Spirit as a voice to guide us. The question, though, is: Are we listening and following the prompts?

I used to have a big problem with anger. A lot of young men are competitive, but I took it to another level. If I or my team didn't win, I blew up. In fact, at a baseball game in high school, I punched my best friend in the face! In Bible college, I played in the student-faculty basketball game at the end of the season. The referee called me for a foul, and when I wouldn't stop arguing, he gave me a technical. That only riled me up even more, so I got another technical, which meant I was out of the game. I went ballistic. I stormed over to the bench, picked up a chair, and in my best Bobby Knight impersonation, threw it onto the court! The students and professors scattered to keep from getting hit. I stomped to the exit door, hit the crash bar, and walked back to my dorm room. And I was studying to be a pastor!

That night, I couldn't sleep. In the morning, I picked up my Bible to read and pray, but before I could even open the book, the Spirit of God pointed out the painful truth: "You have a problem, young man." It was obvious that God wanted me to go to each person and apologize—each member of the faculty, each player on our team, and the referee. I also felt certain God told me that part of my repentance was to avoid any competitive sports for a year.

By the time I met with the third or fourth person, I had my speech down pretty well. It was heartfelt. I was more than embarrassed; I was deeply ashamed. I said, "I'm so sorry for the way I acted. That's not who I want to be. Please forgive me." When

school was out, I went home for the summer. Everybody expected me to join our church's softball team, but I told them, "Not this
year." I wouldn't play a pickup game of basketball, and I wouldn't
even play ping pong.

That year was transforming for me, and much of the anger
dissipated . . . but not all of it. Years later when I was a young pastor, it happened again. I went to a store to buy a pair of shoes. I
found some that were just what I was looking for . . . at a good
price. When I went to the desk to pay for them, the salesman said
the price was much higher than the one listed on the display. I
calmly pointed him to the price on the display, but he said they
weren't exactly the same shoes. We argued, but he didn't budge.
At that point, I went off! I slammed the shoe box on the counter
and yelled, "You're a terrible manager! I'll never shop here ever
again!" As I left the store, I saw some teenagers who had wit-
nessed the whole thing. They cheered for me, and they gave me
high fives. I felt totally vindicated . . . but that night, I couldn't
sleep. The next morning, I sensed the Holy Spirit tell me, "This
isn't who you are, and it's not who you're going to be. You know
what to do." I went back to the store. When the salesman saw me,
he looked like he was getting ready for Round 2, but I told him,
"I blew it. I'm so sorry. I'm a Christian, and that's not how God
wants me to treat people. I was a bad example. Please forgive me."
I bought the shoes for the higher price and walked out.

I wish I could say I've gotten complete victory over my anger, but the kernel of it remained. Several years ago, I got upset
with one of the men on our staff team. As I told my mentor, Sam
Chand, about the situation, I tried to justify my anger. He held up
his hand and said, "Rob, stop right there. Do you remember why
God didn't let Moses into the Promised Land? It wasn't adultery,

and it wasn't embezzling. It was his anger problem. Yours has to stop right here, right now."

As we make the change and keep the change, God gives us plenty of prompts. The problem is that we often don't pay attention, so we miss them. I'm convinced that the Lord is far more active in guiding us than most of us imagine. No, it's not voices or angels or bright lights. He often uses the Scriptures to give us nudges and whispers to warn us, direct us, and affirm the steps we're taking. Sometimes (maybe a lot more than sometimes) the Lord uses our spouse or a close friend to prod us. Before I came to the conclusion that it was time to lose a lot of weight, Becca and I were on vacation, and a nice restaurant had a fantastic buffet. They served the most delicious lamb chops I've ever tasted. I got two, enjoyed them, got two more, devoured them, and then got three more. Becca's withering glare was much louder than words! But somehow, the message didn't penetrate my soul. At the end of the buffet was a dessert tray. After gorging on lamb chops and everything that came with them, I didn't just get a dessert; I took the whole dessert platter to our table—it was huge! When I put it down, Becca put her head down and covered her eyes. I thought, *Cool! I don't have to share with her!* As I look back, I can see hundreds of prompts that I ignored. The problem wasn't that God or Becca weren't communicating with me. The problem was that I wasn't paying attention . . . and even more, I didn't want to hear what they had to say. In addition, during this time my mother had quadruple by-pass surgery, but my thinking was: *That's her, not me.* Did I think about genetics and the possibility that my weight might contribute to a heart problem? Nope, I just kept on eating everything that was put in front of me.

Do you believe God speaks to us? I'm convinced He does, but the real question is: Are our hearts tuned to listen? He speaks in many different ways—primarily through the Scriptures, but also through the Spirit's whispers and nudges, people who care enough to tell us the truth, and circumstances that cause us to sit up and pay closer attention. Jesus wanted us to know that He longs to connect with us in ways that lead us to blessings and spiritual strength. He connected His mission with Psalm 23, one of the most familiar and beloved passages in the Bible: "I am the good shepherd; I know my own sheep, and they know me . . . My sheep listen to my voice; I know them, and they follow me" (John 10:14, 27). God is infinite, and we're not, so there will always be more than a measure of mystery in our relationship with Him, but the principle is clear: God loves to communicate with those He loves . . . people like you and me.

God often uses friends, and sometimes even strangers, to speak into our lives. If we feel loved and safe with people, we'll be able to hear what He's telling us through them, even if it makes us feel uncomfortable or offended. Throughout the Scriptures, we see people stepping up and speaking up to point out a person's need to change course. Thankfully, I have several people who play that role for me (and I have the honor to be one of those people for some others). Others' input may be corrective, instructive, or informative, but if we give them access to our hearts and our lives, we'll be open to whatever they feel they need to tell us. And if we love them, we'll find the courage to say what needs to be said, with a powerful blend of grace and truth so they can really hear us without being defensive.

A lot of people care about us, but they're not sure how to say something that's even a little blunt. To soften the blow, they often use humor. When I was overweight, my sister-in-law from Vietnam sometimes pointed to my bulging stomach and said, "You have baby?" She laughed. I didn't. I wrote her off because I didn't want to think I looked like I was hiding a basketball under my shirt . . . but I did.

Of course, if you only hear God telling you to go around correcting other people, you probably need to listen a lot more! Some of the Spirit's prompts are to perform simple acts of kindness and generosity. You might get a feeling to pay for someone's lunch without them knowing it, take some extra time with someone you would normally pass by quickly, or even make a bigger commitment. How do you know if your impulse to pay for someone's mission trip is from the Lord? Just ask a question or two: Does the person need the money? Do you have the means? Then do it. But are you looking for a parade in your honor if you give it? Think and pray again.

Someone once asked me, "Rob, what about the times that you're wrong about a prompt?"

I replied, "It's never wrong to do a good thing." This gives me permission to take steps of faith and generosity . . . even if sometimes it turns out that my efforts weren't necessary at all. When I take the initiative to care for someone, I'm sure that God is pleased, even if He didn't give me the idea. I can imagine Him saying, "Way to go! You're reflecting My generosity as your Heavenly Father. Keep it up!" For me, this behind-the-scenes interaction with God is the ultimate game within the game. It's very likely no one will know about these exchanges between God and me, but I sure do, and it's a source of life and joy to me . . . and I assume, to God.

"Way to go! You're reflecting My generosity as your Heavenly Father. Keep it up!"

We can cultivate our receptiveness to God's promptings. When someone is whispering softly and we're having trouble hearing them, what do we do? We turn down the noise and pay closer attention. We can do the same thing in our relationship with God. I've found that I'm much more attuned to God's whispers and nudges when I spend time with Him without all the demands and chaos of daily life. And in those times, I don't try to manufacture a prompt. I'm simply open to Him as I read His Word, pray, and reflect on the people and situations of the day.

For many of us, our snap reaction to the Holy Spirit's prompt is to dismiss it: "That can't be!" Instead, it's wise to at least ask, "Could it be?" Certainly, not every thought that comes into our minds is from God, but at least a few are. Wisdom and experience help us sort out the voice of God from the other voices we hear.

RIDE THE WAVE

When sensing the Spirit's prompts becomes a normal part of life, we enter a new, even more exciting phase: riding the wave. This is when we move from vulnerability to stability and find firm footing in vitality. It's like a surfer riding a beautiful, powerful wave. I love to watch surfers on the big waves of the Banzai Pipeline on the North Shore of Oahu, or Mavericks south of San Francisco. They don't start paddling when the wave passes by; they start before it crests so they're already moving and can catch it at just the right moment. When they drop in, the momentum of the wave carries them, and they do all kinds of intricate moves, inside the curl and outside it, which astounds those of us who are watching. In the same way, making a change is a singular decision, but keeping the change is a lifestyle powered by new motivations, new habits, new input, and new payoffs—riding the wave.

Again, surfers have a game within the game. They may be in a tournament or just out for a fun afternoon, but they've learned to read the swells to know if a good wave is coming, move to the place where the wave is most advantageous, anticipate the exact moment to start paddling, and drop in at just the right second. It's thrilling, but it requires practice and skill.

As a young pastor, I was incredibly busy. We had a great staff and wonderful volunteers, but I was trying to juggle ten balls at once. There were so many urgent things that the important ones often got squeezed out. When Connor was seven and Logan was four, I realized I'd been neglecting them . . . not on purpose, but because I felt so much pressure at the church. I was making sure I was home for dinner every night (or almost every night), but our normal rhythm needed to be punctuated with some special times together.

I had to make some major changes in my priorities and my schedule to carve out memorable times for them, time marked in indelible ink on the calendar that was a higher priority than anything else. In other words, if there was any conflict with the dates, the boys came first. We set aside time every quarter to do some fun things together, and nothing was off limits. We visited grandparents for a weekend, went to Disney World, traveled to a beautiful town and went swimming, you name it. At one point, I took them to the Boundary Waters in northern Minnesota, a remote region of beautiful lakes and forests. I lost my phone signal, and the boys cheered! That moment was a loud and powerful message: they longed for me to give them uninterrupted attention . . . totally, absolutely uninterrupted.

To ride this wave of a fresh relationship with Connor and Logan, I let them in on some of what was going on in my work—not too much, but just enough that they felt trusted. Logan told me later that many of their friends didn't even know what their parents did for a living. I wanted our boys to have a picture of what it's like to serve God—the ups and the downs, the thrills and the disappointments. I wanted us to ride the wave together.

I let them know that I couldn't be at all their games because many of the people I needed to meet with were only available in the evenings, but I made sure I was there for the important games and events. When I couldn't be there, we made sure Becca, their grandparents, or one of their uncles showed up. When Connor was ten, I let him pick the place for our family vacation, and when he was thirteen, he picked the country where he and I would visit our missionaries. I gave Logan the same choices. Connor and I went to Swaziland and Mozambique, and Logan and I traveled to Argentina. I believe it was important for their development to let them have this kind of decision-making power, and really, it was a no-lose situation each time.

For me and our family, the game within the game was going beyond the routine to come up with creative ways to connect more deeply. Not long ago, Becca and I asked the boys what moments in our family life has meant the most to them. They talked about enjoying days at Grandpa and Grandma's lake house, hiking in Yellowstone National Park, and other times when we were experiencing each other in a new setting. I wanted to say, "Hey, I spent a lot of money on that trip to Disney! Didn't it even make the list?" No, it didn't. The issue isn't money; it's time, intention, attention, and love.

Before surfers get in the water to paddle out, they make sure their gear is ready. They've looked at the waves and picked the right board, waxed it, put on a wetsuit, and attached the leash. If we're going to ride the wave and catch the momentum of good changes, we need to be prepared, too. One of the most important skills I've learned is also the easiest: I first put every important meeting on my calendar, including my time with Becca and the boys. So, when someone asks me to meet on Thursday at 6:00, I can say, "I'm sorry, but I have something scheduled at that time." I don't have to say that it's dinner with the family, and very, very few people ask what the conflict is. They usually just look for a different time that works for both of us.

Surfers are always pushing themselves and each other to ride a bigger wave and ride more skillfully. In the same way, we need to encourage each other to keep changing, take on bigger challenges, and acquire more skills to conquer them. Our internal push and our willingness to push each other to new heights is the game within the game. Others may only see the changes, but we know what's required behind the scenes to take big steps.

It's unbelievable how much you don't know about the game you've been playing all your life.

—*Mickey Mantle*

CONSIDER THIS:

1. What are some ways you push yourself to set higher goals and achieve more?

2. Who is pushing you, and who are you pushing? What difference does it make to have this kind of relationship?

3. Look again at John 10:14, 27. What are the ways God speaks to you most effectively? What can you do to be more attentive to Him?

4. What are some warning or corrective prompts you've experienced? Where did they originate? How did you respond?

5. What are some encouraging prompts you've received from the Holy Spirit and people who care about you? Again, how did you respond?

6. Are you naturally open to nudges and prompts, or are you suspicious? Has this chapter answered any questions about God's personal involvement in leading you? Explain your answer.

7. What does it (or would it) mean to ride the wave of keeping your changes?

CHAPTER 10

◢ REVISIONING

> For the past 33 years, I have looked in the mirror every morning and asked myself: "If today were the last day of my life, would I want to do what I am about to do today?" And whenever the answer has been no for too many days in a row, I know I need to change something.
>
> —*Steve Jobs*

If individuals, families, and organizations want to make significant changes and keep those changes, they have to reframe their vision—of themselves, each other, their goals, their resources, and their processes. We won't keep our changes if we're still thinking, believing, talking, and acting the way we used to.

Revisioning has become a normal part of my life. I don't resist it, and I don't dread it. I embrace it because it promises a better future. When I decided to lose weight, I had to revision my diet, create a new exercise plan, and change my snacks so they didn't sabotage all the other good choices I was making. When our church began, I had a monumental vision that we would grow to a thousand people. When we hit that number, I didn't just say, "Mission accomplished." We trusted God for a new vision of our church having an ongoing impact on ten thousand people.

Keeping weight off and staying healthy isn't the only new opportunity when we keep the change. I consult with pastors who want to know how God caused our church to grow, how those whose marriages have been saved can become mentors for struggling couples, and how people who have achieved victory over their weight can become health coaches. Whether "health coach" is a formal title or not, all of us who have seen progress can pay it forward. In fact, I believe God gives us both the opportunity and the responsibility to teach what we've learned and impart what we've acquired. Part of what it means to be multiplying disciples is that we pour our hearts and our skills into others. The closeness of this relationship gives us plenty of chances to tell people that the most important truth is that Jesus died the death we should have died, and He lived the life we couldn't live. That's the gospel of grace in a nutshell.

I believe God gives us both the opportunity and the responsibility to teach what we've learned and impart what we've acquired.

I had the wonderful opportunity to play golf with Gary Player, one of the legends of the game. It didn't take long for him to talk to me about the importance of getting in shape and maintaining good health. When I lost weight, I told a lot of people, but Gary's passion for change is off the charts—he's an enthusiastic ambassador for health! He still does a thousand sit-ups every week, and he's very disciplined about his diet. But he doesn't act like this is a dry, lifeless, dull routine. He's excited about the benefits! He's a change agent, and he tells everyone who will listen . . . and some who don't want to listen. When we made the turn from the ninth to the tenth hole, he walked up to a woman and her overweight son, and he told her, "Ma'am, I know you love your son, but he really needs to lose weight. Don't give him dessert, and give him smaller portions. It'll change his life. Trust me." The look on her face showed that she was equally dumbfounded, insulted, and encouraged. When Gary walked away, he had given her a shaft of light on her son and his future, and it was up to her to decide what to do with it.

EBENEZER

When the people of Israel wanted to mark major progress, they set up "stones of remembrance." For instance, when the day finally arrived for God's people to cross the Jordan River and enter the Promised Land, Joshua wanted to be sure no one would forget what God had done.

When all the people had crossed the Jordan, the Lord said to Joshua, "Now choose twelve men, one from each tribe. Tell them, 'Take twelve stones from the very place where the priests are standing in the middle of the Jordan. Carry them out and pile them up at the place where you will camp tonight.'"

So Joshua called together the twelve men he had chosen—one from each of the tribes of Israel. He told them, "Go into the middle of the Jordan, in front of the Ark of the Lord your God. Each of you must pick up one stone and carry it out on your shoulder—twelve stones in all, one for each of the twelve tribes of Israel. We will use these stones to build a memorial. In the future your children will ask you, 'What do these stones mean?' Then you can tell them, 'They remind us that the Jordan River stopped flowing when the Ark of the Lord's Covenant went across.' These stones will stand as a memorial among the people of Israel forever." (Joshua 4:1-7)

We need to remember times when God has given us great blessings, and we need to remember when God has saved our skins. Many years after the crossing of the Jordan, during the time of the judges, Samuel led the people against the Philistines, a much stronger force. Things looked bleak for the Israelites, but then something amazing happened:

> Just as Samuel was sacrificing the burnt offering, the Philistines arrived to attack Israel. But the Lord spoke with a mighty voice of thunder from heaven that day, and the Philistines were thrown into such confusion that the Israelites defeated them. The men of Israel chased them from Mizpah to a place below Beth-car, slaughtering them all along the way.
>
> Samuel then took a large stone and placed it between the towns of Mizpah and Jeshanah. He named it Ebenezer (which means "the stone of help"), for he said, "Up to this point the Lord has helped us!" (1 Samuel 7:10-12)

I'm sure Gary is thrilled when he hears stories of people who have taken his advice and made the changes, and he's filled with even more satisfaction when they tell him they've helped others. Telling our story of progress gives us a shot of endorphins, hormones that relieve pain and flood us with a sense of satisfaction. They're called "feel-good" chemicals . . . and they require no prescription! We need to look in the rearview mirror fairly often to see how far we've come. I keep pictures on my phone of my "fat Rob" driver's license and me walking on the beach with my massive gut. I show the pictures to people and say, "Look at this. Sometimes I can't believe that was me." I get a shot of joy and energy, and at least a few people are encouraged to take their first steps. My pictures are my stones of remembrance, my Ebenezer. Who needs to be reminded? I certainly do, and they give a graphic depiction to others about God's grace, wisdom, and strength in my life.

Do you have an Ebenezer or two? I know a man who keeps a piece of metal on his shelf at home. It's from his car when he crashed it when he was drunk, and he often looks at it to remember how close he came to losing everything, including his life, but God gave him a second chance. A couple has two intertwined wedding rings framed and hung on a wall in their home. They explained that they came very close to a divorce, and when God brought them back together, they got new rings. The old ones are a symbol of what they almost lost but what was gloriously restored.

It doesn't take a lot of money to create an environment that tells meaningful stories—just some thought and creativity. Our homes need to tell the stories that are most important to us through pictures and other mementos of turning-point events and people who mean the world to us. When we see them, we remember; when others see them, we can tell them the stories.

The folded American flag in my office is from my father's funeral. I have the certificate from the Billy Graham Association when I trusted in Jesus, made out to Robby Ketterling. A bowling pin in my office reminds me that my grandfather started his career as a pinsetter in a bowling alley—it doesn't get much more behind-the-scenes and humble than that. When people ask about it, I tell them the story of my grandfather, and how I'm the first person on that side of the family to go to college.

In his book, *From Tablet to Table*, Leonard Sweet explains that the dinner table is a place where families can (and should) regularly refer to stones of remembrance: "At the table, where food and stories are passed from one person to another and one generation to another, is where each of us learns who we are, where we come from, what we can be, to whom we belong, and to what we are called."[28] Our stories shape young lives.

From time to time, I need to review the list of what I've gained by keeping the change:

> I survived a heart attack.

> I have more energy.

> I think more clearly.

> I feel better about the way I look.

> I'm not short of breath when I walk up a flight of stairs.

> I've gained credibility to give advice as a pastor.

> I have great stories to tell instead of just complaining about what's gone wrong.

> My obedience in one area spills over into obedience in other areas.

> ❯ I'm excited, not threatened, when I hear about others who are making real progress.

> ❯ I'm very seldom apathetic or indifferent.

> ❯ I'm hungry for more of what God has in store for me.

> ❯ Our whole family has learned to tell great stories to each other.

These statements help me remember the *why*—the motivation for making and keeping change. It's not just to check something off a to-do list, and it's not to impress anybody. Pursuing God's best for me and my family is leaving a legacy for the people I love.

DON'T STOP HALFWAY

I know some people who are "miserably saved." They're Christians, but something is holding them back from being fully devoted to Jesus. They may make some small changes, but they quickly revert to their previous lifestyle. In fact, some of them glory in the way things used to be. A miserably saved alcoholic's identity is based in how much he used to drink and the crazy people he ran around with. "You should have known me back then!" he brags. This is remembering the past, but not in a good way. To some extent, they still see their past as "the good old days." It's almost as if they wish they could go back, but their commitment to sobriety won't let them.

But others are haunted by the past. They have trouble disengaging from it, but not because it's so attractive. Their past hurts were so traumatic that the wounds are still open and sore.

For both—those who glory in the past and those who can't shake free from it—the solution is the same: don't stop halfway. God has so much more for all of us—a new identity as beloved children of God, a new source of strength and hope, and a new set of relationships with people who see great potential in our future.

God has so much more for all of us—a new identity as beloved children of God, a new source of strength and hope, and a new set of relationships with people who see great potential in our future.

When we read the Apostle Paul's letters to Timothy, we get a hint that the young man had some struggles with self-doubt. Again and again, Paul tried to put warmth in Timothy's heart and steel in his soul. In his last letter, written shortly before his death, Paul encouraged Timothy: "This is why I remind you to fan into flames the spiritual gift God gave you when I laid my hands on you. For God has not given us a spirit of fear and timidity, but of power, love, and self-discipline" (2 Timothy 1:6-7). Later in that letter, he added:

> But you, Timothy, certainly know what I teach, and how I live, and what my purpose in life is. You know my faith, my patience, my love, and my endurance. . . . But you must remain faithful to the things you have been taught. You know they are true, for you know you can trust

those who taught you. You have been taught the holy
Scriptures from childhood, and they have given you the
wisdom to receive the salvation that comes by trusting in
Christ Jesus. All Scripture is inspired by God and is use-
ful to teach us what is true and to make us realize what
is wrong in our lives. It corrects us when we are wrong
and teaches us to do what is right. God uses it to prepare
and equip his people to do every good work. (2 Timothy
3:10, 14-17)

When I read these letters, I imagine Paul writing those things
to me: "Rob, fan the flames of spiritual fire. Don't let the embers
cool! If you're afraid, that's not how God wants you to respond.
His Spirit will give you the courage to overcome your fear and follow Him wherever He leads. And Rob, you know God's purpose
for you. Live in it. Live out of it. Share it with everyone you know.
You've had great mentors. Trust what they've built into you. And
stay in the Word. That's how God speaks to you, redirects you,
and equips you to be all He has called you to be. And one more
thing: Rob, I believe God wants to do great things in you and
through you. Trust Him and go for it!"

I think Paul would write something like that to you, too.

DON'T FORGET TO REMEMBER

Without regular and meaningful reminders, we run the risk
of losing the change. We drift back into old habits, old patterns of
thinking, and old temptations to slide even further. We not only
lose the progress we've made, we also lose the joy, the sense of
God's smile, and our credibility with people who are watching us.

We're never motionless. We're always either moving forward or backward. Isaac Newton's first law of physics is that an object in motion will continue in motion unless a force acts to change it. That's true in the spiritual, relational, and psychological world, too. The problem for us is that we live with three sources of constant pressure dragging on our forward motion. The *lure of our culture*—power, pleasure, possessions, and popularity—is the air we breathe and the water where we swim. Our *fallen nature* is still with us, and it always leans toward selfishness. And *the enemy of our souls* uses temptation, deception, and accusation to get us off track.

If you'll indulge me another *Matrix* scene . . . Cypher takes the red pill and sees the truth underlying the simulated reality as it appears on the surface. Now, he has second thoughts. He sees a huge, juicy steak, and the temptation is overwhelming. He laments, "I know this steak doesn't exist. I know that when I put it in my mouth, the Matrix is telling my brain that it is juicy and delicious. After nine years, you know what I realize? Ignorance is bliss." When I watch this scene, my mouth waters. I can almost taste the steak! That's a picture of the temptations we experience all around us. They promise joy, power, and pleasure, but it's all an elaborate illusion. But ignorance isn't bliss. Something else is very real: God's heart for us, His love for all people, and our place in His kingdom as His partners in the family enterprise of reaching and rescuing the world from sin.

One of our main problems is that we take too much credit for our progress, and we forget the role God has played. Let me be clear: salvation is all God—He draws us close, He opens the eyes of our hearts, He shows us our helplessness apart from Christ, and He gives us faith to believe. It's all about Him. But spiritual growth is a partnership between God and us.

Paul put it this way: "Work hard to show the results of your salvation, obeying God with deep reverence and fear. For God is working in you, giving you the desire and the power to do what pleases him" (Philippians 2:12-13). Interestingly, this comes immediately after the beautiful passage about Christ humbling himself to become one of us so He could die in our place to pay the penalty for our sins. Now, Paul reminds us that out of appreciation for what Jesus has done to us, for us, and in us, we work hard to make progress and make a difference, trusting God to give us right motives and strength. The Spirit prompts, guides, and empowers; we follow and obey.

It's human nature to have memory lapses. We often forget the things we need to remember, and we remember the things we should forget. The encouraging, hopeful, inspiring memories fade, but flashbacks of failure and shame seem all too real. For the toxic thoughts, we need "intentional amnesia."

We often forget the things we need to remember, and we remember the things we should forget.

In good times and bad, we can quickly forget God and feel that we're on our own. Solomon wrote, "For if I grow rich, I may deny you and say, 'Who is the Lord?' And if I am too poor, I may steal and thus insult God's holy name" (Proverbs 30:9). Think you're exempt from forgetting God in the good times and blaming God in your struggles? Think again. It happens to all of us . . . unless we build reminders into our lives.

The Jewish festivals reinforced positive memories for the nation, for families, and for individuals, and they included children so they'd learn the history and traditions. Passover celebrates God's deliverance of His people from slavery in Egypt. On the night of the last plague, when the angel of death would be sent to kill all the firstborn, God told His people to sacrifice a lamb and put the blood on the doorposts and lintel of their homes so the angel would pass over them. Today, one of the traditions of Passover is having the youngest child ask, "Why does this night differ from all other nights?" The answer is recited in unison by all those present.

Pentecost, celebrated on the fifth weekend after Passover, is associated with two important events, one ancient and one current: God giving the Law to Moses at Sinai, and thanksgiving for the first part of the wheat harvest.

The Feast of Tabernacles (or Booths) takes place in the fall when the major harvest is brought in, as well as celebrating the exodus from Egypt when people stayed in portable tents as they traveled.

The eight days of Hanukkah commemorate the Jewish people's victory over the Greek tyrant, Antiochus Epiphanes, in the second century before Christ. The candles represent the rededication of the temple in Jerusalem, which had been desecrated by the oppressive Greek ruler.

I was privileged to take my mother to Israel, and we were in Jerusalem on a Sabbath day. We observed the day by just walking around the town, watching the people, and talking about what we were seeing. I didn't answer any emails, and I didn't text anyone.

It was a day to soak up the place where so much of our faith's history took place. At the end of the day, my mother looked at me and said, "This is one of the happiest days of my life. It's just the two of us, and it's wonderful." Recurring joy is another benefit of recalling the stories we've lived with those we love.

The Jewish people have something many of us don't. In America, we celebrate Thanksgiving, but it has largely become the starting gun for panic shopping, and Christmas is often far more about the gifts than the Giver. We may not want to bring back the major Jewish holidays, but we can certainly create traditions in our families that point us more powerfully to God's goodness and greatness.

IT'S WORTH IT

If you're wondering if keeping the change is worth the trouble to revision a better future, to resist temptation and overcome excuses, and to trust God to do what only He can do, let me assure you: It's 100 percent worth it! New thinking and new habits always feel awkward at first, but we need to remember the principle of the flywheel. The huge wheel takes a lot of effort to get it moving, but continuing to apply the same amount of force causes it to turn faster and faster. In other words, you may not see dramatic progress at the beginning, but if you stick with it, you'll fly! Your sense of vitality, your relationships, and your impact on others will be far bigger and better than you ever thought possible.

And if your flywheel is moving pretty fast, look for people around you who are just starting to make and keep change, and give theirs a push to help them get going. Sooner or later, you'll be able to look back and see that God has used you to change the trajectory of the people you love . . . and maybe some you don't even know.

Paul spent three weeks in the Greek city of Thessalonica, teaching and preaching to everyone who would listen. Then he moved on to Corinth to tell people about Jesus. At one point, he sent Timothy back to find out how the church plant was doing. Timothy reported to Paul that there were some struggles among the believers, but overall, they were walking with God and serving faithfully. After Timothy's report, Paul wrote his first letter to the believers in Thessalonica, and he poured out his gratitude that they had made major changes and were keeping the change. Then Paul encouraged them to "excel still more" (1 Thessalonians 4:1 NASB1995). I'm pretty sure that would be Paul's message to those of us who are trying hard to walk with God and continuing to pursue His best for us. And that's my message to you at the end of this book: Yes, you have struggles. Keeping the change requires faith and tenacity, but you're doing it. Don't stop. Don't even slow down. You've worked so hard for this change, so do everything you can to keep it!

CONSIDER THIS:

1. What characteristics does it take to be a change agent? Is there a certain personality type that fits this profile? Why or why not?

2. What are some mementos, "stones of remembrance," you have in your house or at your office? What is the message in each one? If you don't have enough, what are some you can identify and display?

3. What are the stories you need to remember, and what are some others that need you to practice intentional amnesia? What difference will these choices make?

4. What will you lose if you forget to remember the benefits of tenacity and trusting God's faithfulness?

5. If Paul wrote you a letter today, what do you think he'd write? How would you respond?

6. What is the one key point you'll take away from this book? How will you apply it? What difference will it make?

◢ ENDNOTES

1   "Coronary Collaterals," American Heart Association, https://www.ahajournals.org/doi/10.1161/01.cir.0000065118.99409.5f

2   For more about this awkward dinner conversation and its impact on me, see the introduction of my book, *Change Before You Have To*, available at River Valley Resources.

3   Srinivas Rao, "96% of People Fail When They Try to Better Themselves—Here Are 3 Ways to Make Sure You Don't," *Business Insider*, March 4, 2017, https://www.businessinsider.com/96-of-people-fail-when-they-try-to-better-themselves-here-are-3-ways-to-make-sure-you-dont-2017-3

4   Brent Gleason, "1 Reason Why Most Change Management Efforts Fail," *Forbes*, June 25, 2017, https://www.forbes.com/sites/brentgleeson/2017/07/25/1-reason-why-most-change-management-efforts-fail/?sh=cc67a9b546b7

5   Ashley Stahl, "This New Year's Set Goals, Not Resolutions," *Forbes*, December 9, 2021, https://www.forbes.com/sites/ashleystahl/2021/12/09/this-new-years-set-goals-not-resolutions/?sh=5384bc7c1ece

6   Cited in *Summa Theologica* by Thomas Aquinas, https://www.ccel.org/ccel/aquinas/summa.SS_Q158_A8.html

7   A quote from John Chrysostom in Tim Keller's sermon, "The Healing of Anger."

8   *Leadership and Self-Deception*, The Arbinger Institute (San Francisco: Berrett-Koehler Publishers, 2010), p. xi.

9   Brené Brown, *The Gifts of Imperfection* (New York: Random House, 2020), p. 15.

10 Kathy Caprino, "5 Core Reasons People Resist Facing Reality Instead of Changing It," *Forbes*, April 28, 2017, https://www.forbes.com/sites/kathycaprino/2017/04/28/5-core-reasons-people-resist-facing-reality-instead-of-changing-it/?sh=70c-b387e7e23

11 "The Social Dilemma: Social Media and Your Mental Health," McLean, Harvard Medical School, January 21, 2022, https://www.mcleanhospital.org/essential/it-or-not-social-medias-affecting-your-mental-health

12 Ron Carucci, "4 Ways Lying Becomes the Norm at a Company," *Harvard Business Review*, February 15, 2019, https://hbr.org/2019/02/4-ways-lying-becomes-the-norm-at-a-company

13 Corrie ten Boom, *The Hiding Place* (Grand Rapids: Chosen Books, 1971), p. 8.

14 These observations about the Beatitudes are adapted from "The Norms of the Kingdom" by Tim Keller, https://podcast.gospelinlife.com/e/the-norms-of-the-kingdom/

15 The term is widely used today. It was coined in the 1950s by British pediatrician and psychologist Donald W. Winnicott.

16 "Good Good Father," wcicfm.org, https://www.wcicfm.org/song/good-good-father/

17 Madeline Dangerfield-Cha and Joy Zhang, "Solving the Loneliness Epidemic, Two Generations at a Time," *Stanford Social Innovation Review*, March 29, 2021, https://ssir.org/articles/entry/solving_the_loneliness_epidemic_two_generations_at_a_time

18 Evan Andrews, "Did a Premature Obituary Inspire the Nobel Prize?" *History*, July 23, 2020, https://www.history.com/news/did-a-premature-obituary-inspire-the-nobel-prize

19 Dave Ramsey, "How the Debt Snowball Method Works," Ramsey Solutions, September 29, 2021, https://www.ramseysolutions.com/debt/how-the-debt-snowball-method-works

20 James Clear, "5 Common Mistakes that Cause New Habits to Fail," https://jamesclear.com/habits-fail

21 William Barclay, *The Letters of James and Peter* (Louisville: Westminster John Knox Press, 1958), p. 99.

22 Arthur Brooks, "A Gentler, Better Way to Change Minds," *The Atlantic,* April 7, 2022, https://www.theatlantic.com/family/archive/2022/04/arguing-with-someone-different-values/629495/

23 Logan Ketterling, "Don't Post That," June 25, 2020, https://www.youtube.com/watch?v=fKUjH9oZ9po

24 Bessel Van Der Kolk, M.D., "Childhood Trauma Leads to Brains Wired for Fear" and *The Body Keeps the Score* (New York: Penguin Publishing Group, 2014), p. 3.

25 Tim Keller, *Walking with God through Pain and Suffering* (New York: Penguin Publishing Group, 2015), p. 9.

26 Charles Haddon Spurgeon, *Spurgeon's Sermons Volume 2*, edited by Anthony Uyl, (Ontario: Devoted Publishing, 1856), p. 238.

27 Adapted from "5 Reasons People Resist Change and What We Can Do about It," Daniella Whyte, *Inc.,* https://www.inc.com/daniella-whyte/5-reasons-people-resist-change-and-what-we-can-do-about-it.html

28 Leonard Sweet, *From Tablet to Table* (Colorado Springs: NavPress, 2014), p. 8.

◢ *USING* KEEP THE CHANGE *IN* CLASSES AND GROUPS

Keep the Change is designed for individual study, small groups, and classes. The best way to absorb and apply these principles is for each person to individually study and answer the questions at the end of each chapter, and then discuss them in a group environment.

Order enough copies of the book for each person to have a copy. For couples, encourage both to have their own book so they can record their individual reflections.

A recommended schedule for a small group or class might be:

WEEK 1

Introduce the material. As a group leader, tell your story of experiencing meaningful relationships, share your hopes for the group, and provide books for each person. Encourage people to read the assigned chapter each week and answer the questions. For the next week, have them read the Introduction and Chapter 1.

WEEKS 2–11

Each week, introduce the topic for the week and share a story of how God has used the principles in your life. Lead people through a discussion of the questions at the end of the chapter.

Personalize Each Lesson

Don't feel pressured to cover every question in your group discussions. Pick out three or four that had the biggest impact on you, and focus on those, or ask people in the group to share their responses to the questions that meant the most to them that week.

Make sure you personalize the principles and applications. At least once in each group meeting, add your own story to illustrate a particular point.

Make the Scriptures come alive. Far too often, we read the Bible like it's a phone book, with little or no emotion. Paint a vivid picture for people. Provide insights about the risk and the power of authentic relationships, and help those in your group sense the emotions of specific people in each scene.

Focus on Application

The questions at the end of each chapter and your encouragement to group members to be authentic will help your group take big steps to apply the principles they're learning. Share how you are applying the principles in particular chapters each week, and encourage them to take steps of growth, too.

Three Types of Questions

If you've led groups for a few years, you already understand the importance of using open questions to stimulate discussion. Three types of questions are *limiting, leading,* and *open.* Many of the questions at the end of each lesson are open questions.

Limiting questions focus on an obvious answer, such as, "What does Jesus call himself in John 10:11?" They don't stimulate reflection or discussion. If you want to use questions like these, follow them with thought-provoking, open questions.

Leading questions require the listener to guess what the leader has in mind, such as, "Why did Jesus use the metaphor of a shepherd in John 10?" (He was probably alluding to a passage in Ezekiel, but many people don't know that.) The teacher who asks a leading question has a definite answer in mind. Instead of asking this kind of question, you should just teach the point and perhaps ask an open question about the point you have made.

Open questions usually don't have right or wrong answers. They stimulate thinking, and they are far less threatening because the person answering doesn't risk ridicule for being wrong. These questions often begin with "Why do you think . . .?" or "What are some reasons that . . .?" or "How would you have felt in that situation?"

Preparation

As you prepare to teach this material in a group, consider these steps:

1. Carefully and thoughtfully read the book. Make notes, highlight key sections, quotes, or stories, and complete the reflection section at the end of each chapter. This will familiarize you with the entire scope of the content.

2. As you prepare for each week's group, read the corresponding chapter again and make additional notes.

3. Tailor the amount of content to the time allotted. You may not have time to cover all the questions, so pick the ones that are most pertinent.

4. Add your own stories to personalize the message and add impact.

5. Before and during your preparation, ask God to give you wisdom, clarity, and power. Trust him to use your group to change people's lives.

6. Most people will get far more out of the group if they read the chapter and complete the reflection each week. Order books before the group or class begins or after the first week.

◢ ABOUT THE AUTHOR

As Lead Pastor of River Valley Church, Rob Ketterling is highly regarded for his vision and relentless passion to expand the kingdom of God.

He and his wife Becca have been married for over thirty years and launched River Valley Church in 1995, which has since grown to minister to around 10,000 people each weekend across nine locations in the Minneapolis, Minnesota, area and one international campus (Mbekelweni, eSwatini).

Rob has a down-to-earth preaching style, allowing his audience to take practical steps in their journey no matter where they are. He inspires people to live an authentic, faith-filled relationship with Jesus, and he challenges leaders at every level to change the world. He is the author of several books, including *Change Before You Have To*, *Front Row Leadership*, and *Speed of Unity*. He currently serves on the Lead Team of the Association of Related Churches (ARC) and the Church Multiplication Network (CMN). In addition to church planting, Rob's heart bleeds for global missions. Since founding River Valley Church, the church has given over $50 million to missions efforts around the world.

Rob loves traveling and spending time with Becca and his family. Rob and Becca have two sons, Connor and Logan, both on staff at River Valley Church, and two daughter-in-laws Alexia and Mikayla. When Rob isn't at work building the kingdom, he's recharging on the golf course.

DO YOU WANT MORE *LEADERSHIP INSIGHT* FROM ROB KETTERLING?

We started the River Valley Network to help churches become healthy and generous. We are consistently adding new resources and training opportunities for you and your team. We want to see the local church thrive all over the world and see the Kingdom of God move forward! I hope you will be a part of it.

Rob Ketterling

RIVER VALLEY
NETWORK

River Valley Network exists to teach and inspire every church to accelerate their health and generosity to supernatural levels. We do this through:

ANNUAL RIVER VALLEY CONFERENCE

Hosted for pastors to be poured into and refreshed through worship, teachings, and breakout sessions to continue the mission in which they are called.

GENEROSITY ACCELERATORS

One-day events to teach and inspire churches to increase generosity in their church to supernatural levels.

ROUNDTABLES

Throughout the year, we offer roundtables in specific ministry areas such as Creative, NextGen, and Church Operations.

TALKING CHURCH PODCAST

Hosted by River Valley Network, you will learn from ministry leaders on a variety of subjects, develop your leadership skills, and break new growth barriers!

We are passionate about generosity because we believe a generous church should be the only type of church. Together, with generous hearts, we will see more churches planted, more missionaries sent, and the message of Jesus spread like never before!

VISIT RIVERVALLEYNETWORK.ORG TO LEARN MORE AND SUBSCRIBE TO OUR WEEKLY UPDATE FOR ADDITIONAL RESOURCES.

◢ RESOURCES

To order more copies of
Keep the Change or any of the resources listed below, go to
resources.rivervalley.org

216

ALSO BY ROB KETTERLING:

SPEED OF UNITY

The Blue Angels and the Thunderbirds perform incredible feats of aeronautics, but only because their minds, hearts, and bodies are perfectly synchronized. In the same way, leaders get the most out of their teams when they raise the level of unity. In this book, Rob's principles and advice will challenge you and inspire you to fight for a new speed, the *Speed of Unity*. This is only achieved when people are intentionally invested in the success of the team, not just individual accomplishments. Hang on. It's going to be a fast ride!

FIX IT!
WHOSE PROBLEM IS IT?

ROB KETTERLING

FIX IT! WHOSE PROBLEM IS IT?

Even before the smoke starts to rise, every leader sees the signals that something isn't right. Your wide variety of problems may vary in severity, scope, and timing, but they have one thing in common: People are looking to you to fix them all!

But before you go running for the fire extinguisher, the duct tape, or to schedule an emergency meeting of your board of elders, see what Pastor Rob Ketterling has to say. It may surprise you to discover that the problem isn't yours to fix.

With wisdom acquired through personal experience and no shortage of trial and error (which he shares with brutal honesty and a large dose of humor), Ketterling will verify that some problems are indeed yours to handle. Other times, however, it's best to delegate the matter to "them" (your staff, lay leaders, volunteers, or whomever), or you risk denying others valuable opportunities to learn and grow. And sometimes, nothing less than a "big boom" from God will resolve a dilemma. The key is to learn which route to take in every situation.

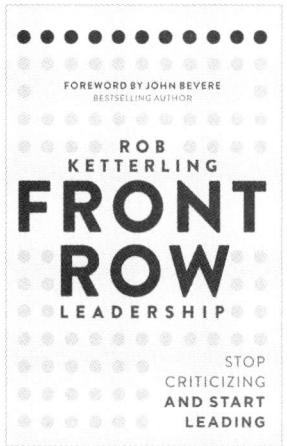

FRONT ROW LEADERSHIP

Become the person of influence you were born to be. Whether you're a CEO, a volunteer, or a homemaker, leadership is your responsibility. Rob Ketterling offers tools that will empower you to move up to the front and lead the change you want to see take place. Learn to engage the leadership process and contribute with your God-given strengths.

THRILL SEQUENCE

Are you constantly looking for your next adrenaline-packed experience? Seeking another dose of excitement from an adventure with suspense, fun, and danger rolled into one? What if your Christian life were just as thrilling? Rob Ketterling encourages readers to seek adventure in a full-on, reignited faith. He challenges others to discover the excitement in passionately pursuing a life of service and reckless faith.

CHANGE BEFORE YOU HAVE TO

What will it take for you to change? For most of us, it takes a crisis, a tragedy, a pain so great that change is actually forced upon us. By then, it's way too late. But what if you could find the strength to change before the pain, before the crisis, before the tragedy? No more excuses, no more good intentions, it's time to change and live life to the fullest!